DRIVE FAST
DON'T STOP

BOOK THIRTEEN
LOS ANGELES & PALM SPRINGS

PALM SPRINGS

PALM SPRINGS

PALM SPRINGS

PALM SPRINGS

PALM SPRINGS

PALM SPRINGS

LOS ANGELES

LOS ANGELES

LOS ANGELES

LOS ANGELES

LOS ANGELES

LOS ANGELES

CALIFORNIA

CALIFORNIA

CALIFORNIA

CALIFORNIA

CALIFORNIA

CALIFORNIA

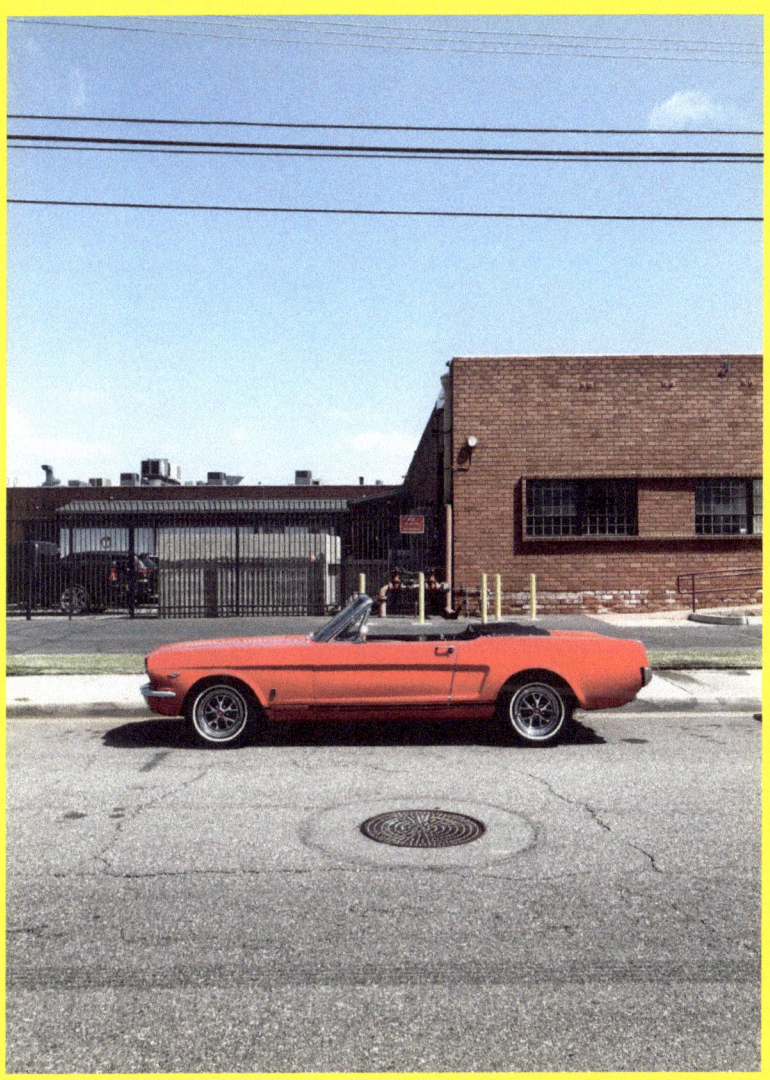

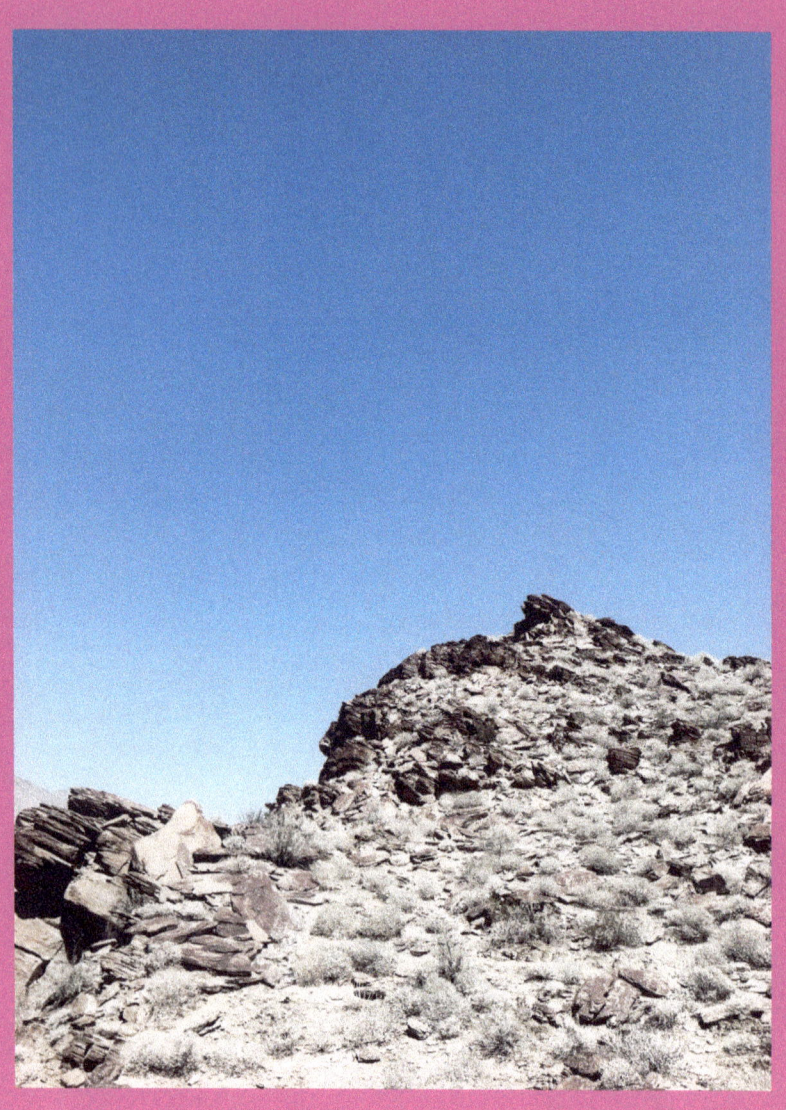

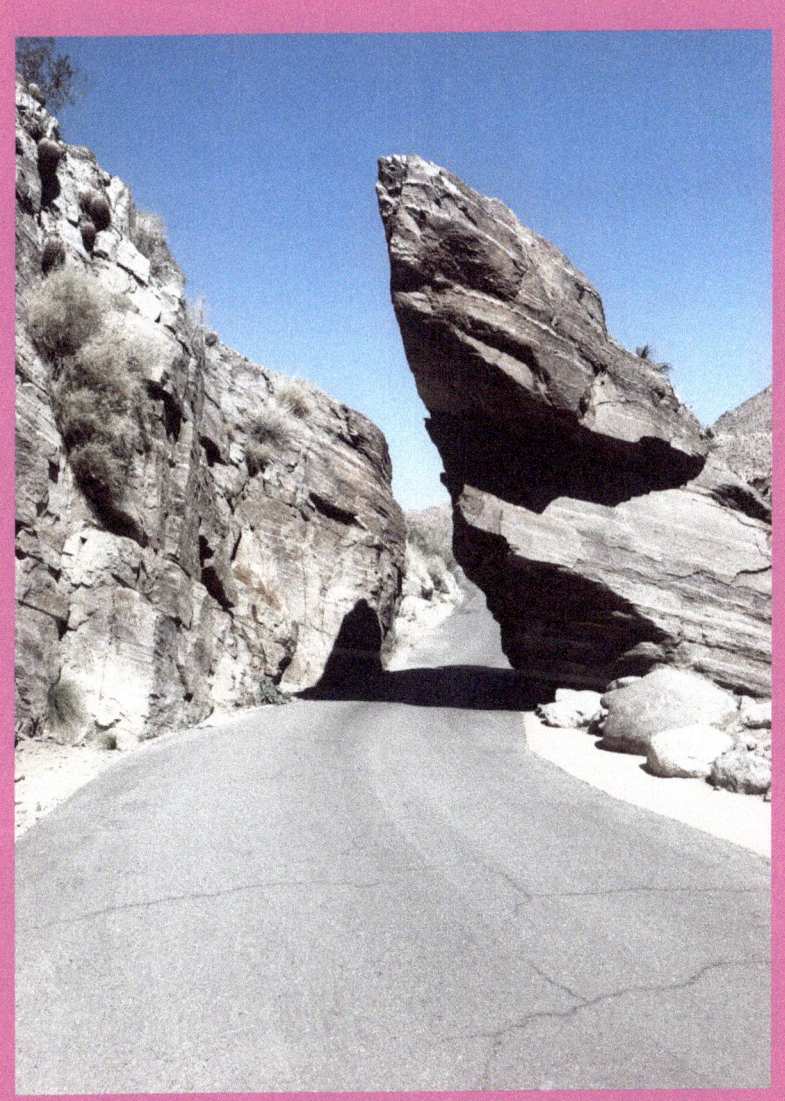

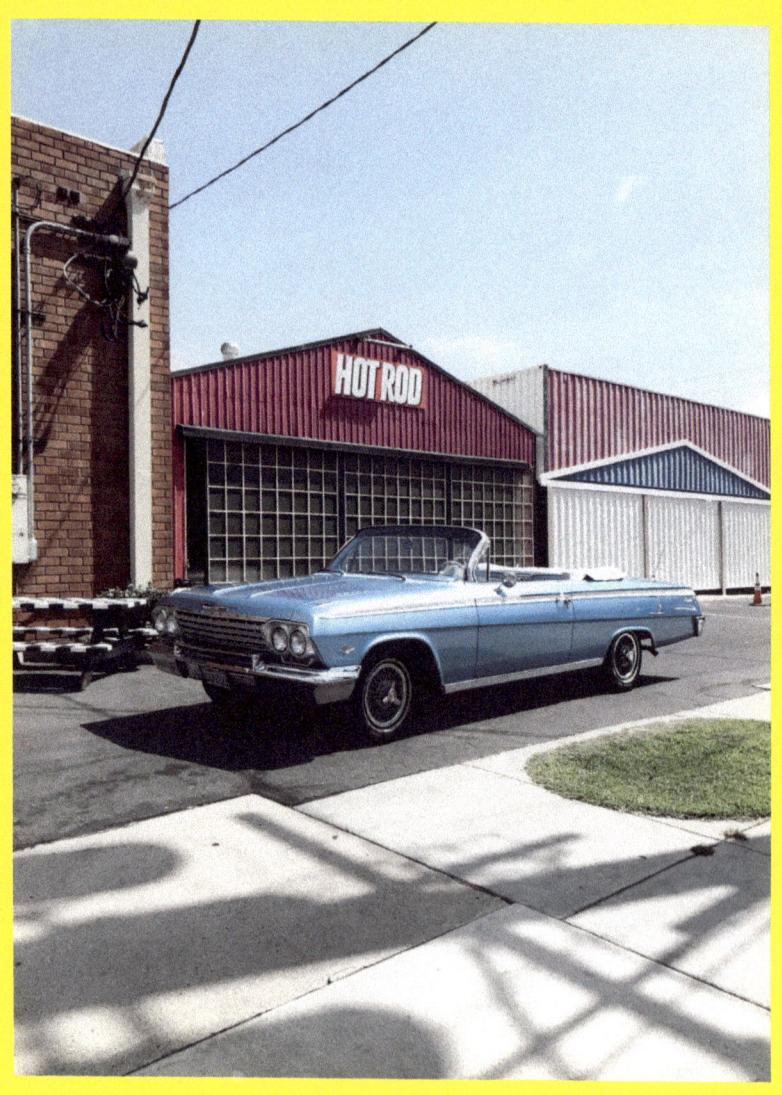

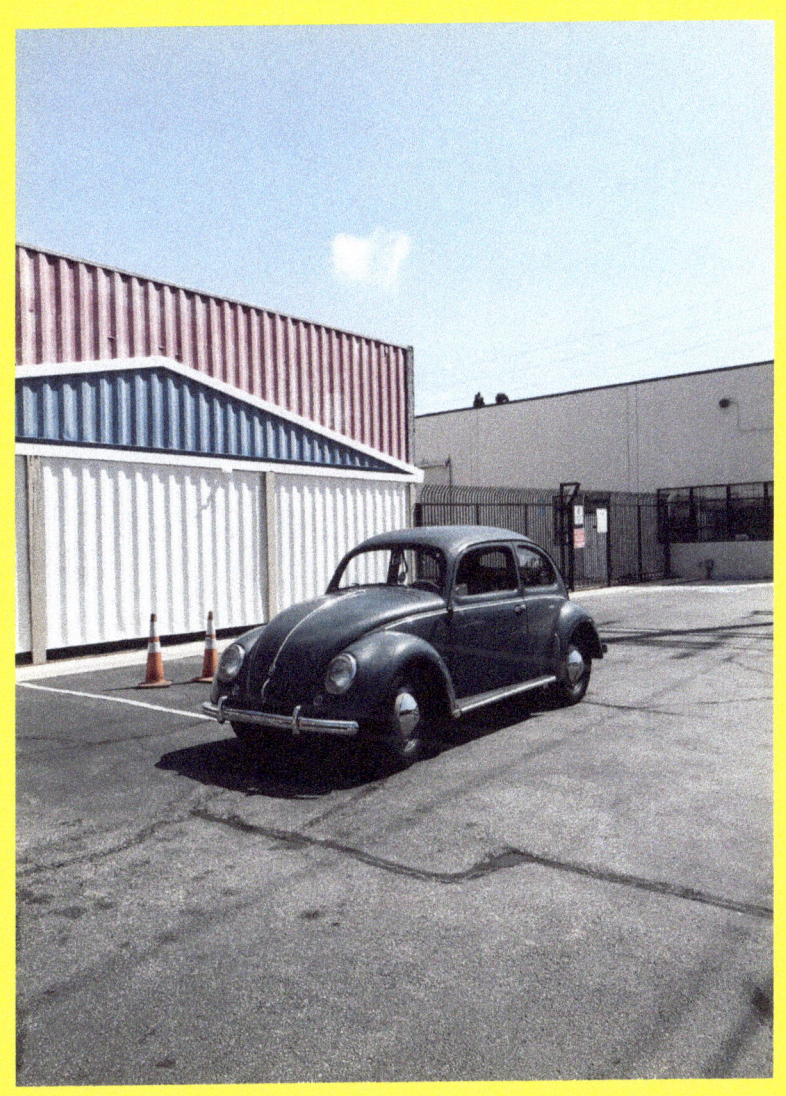

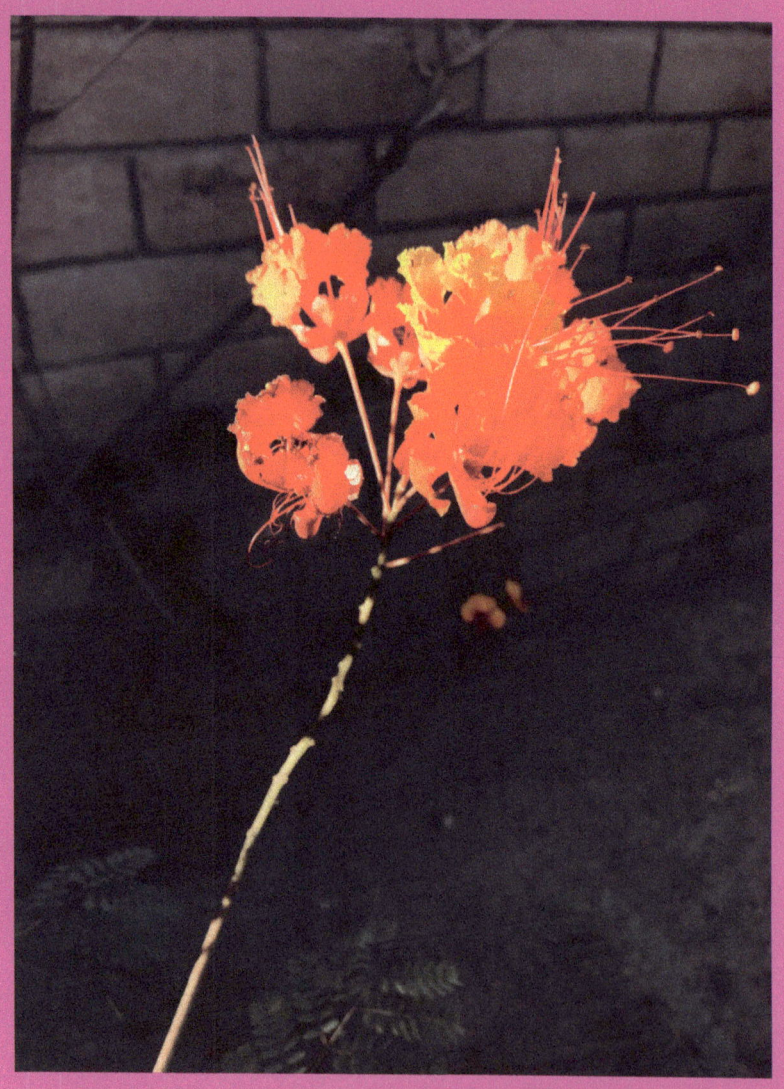

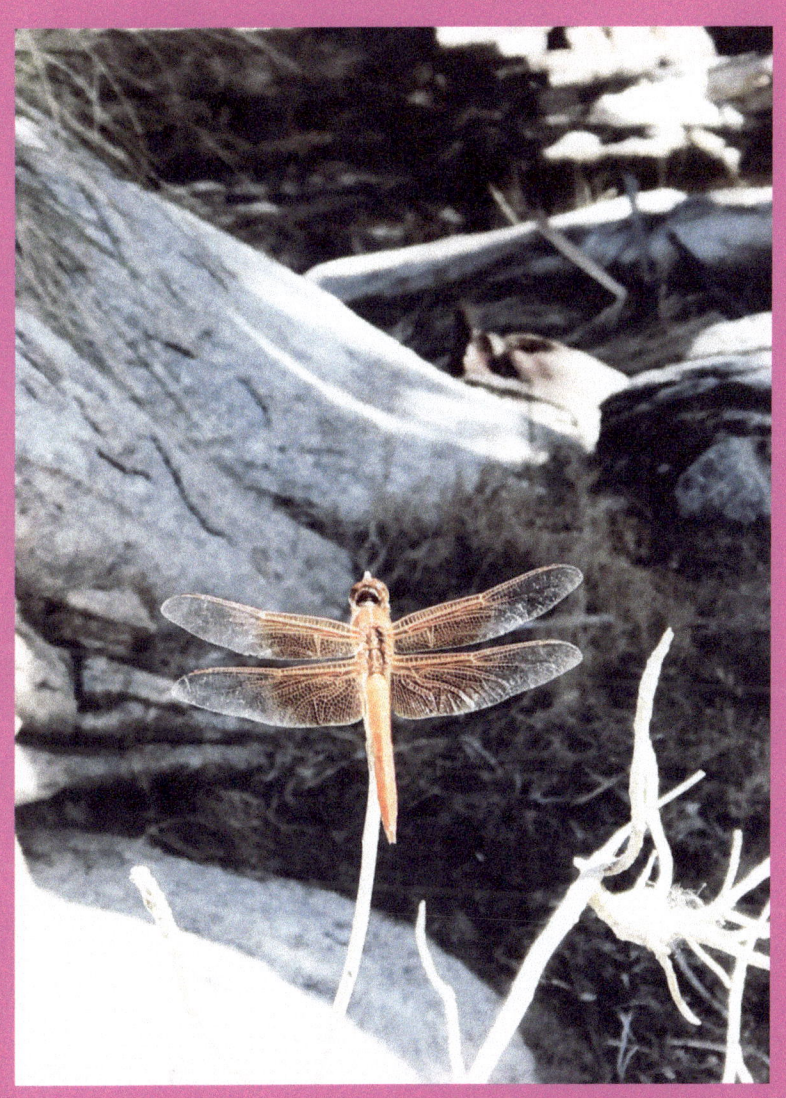

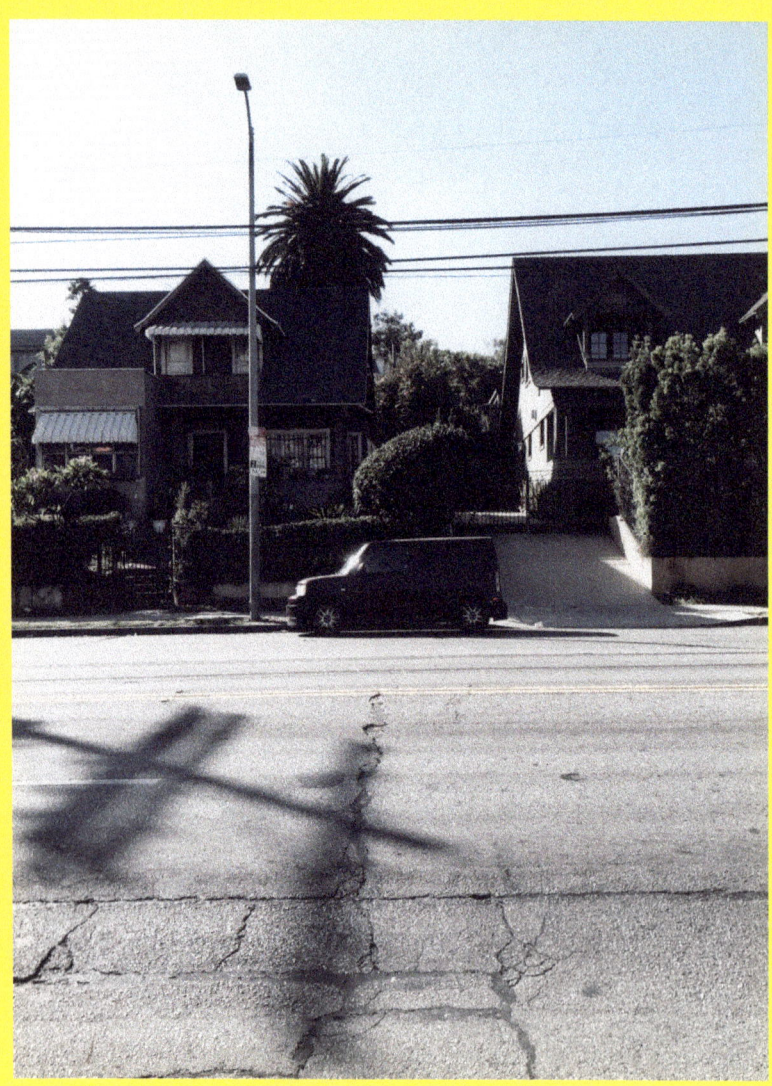

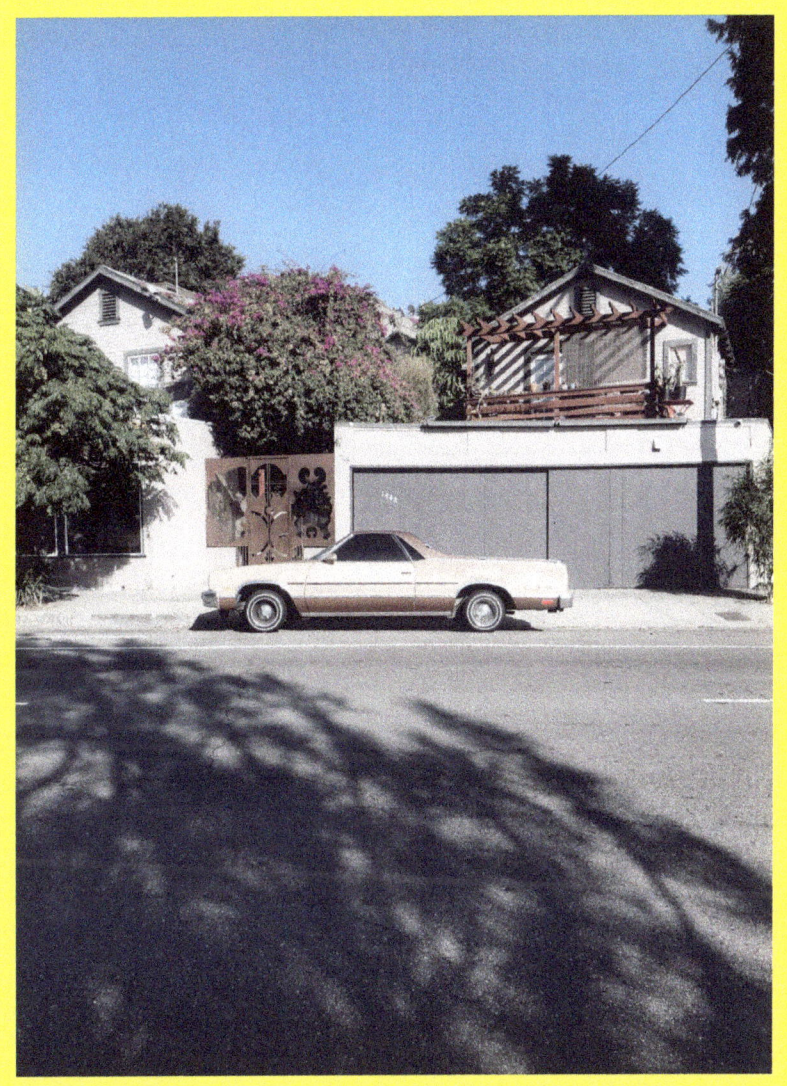

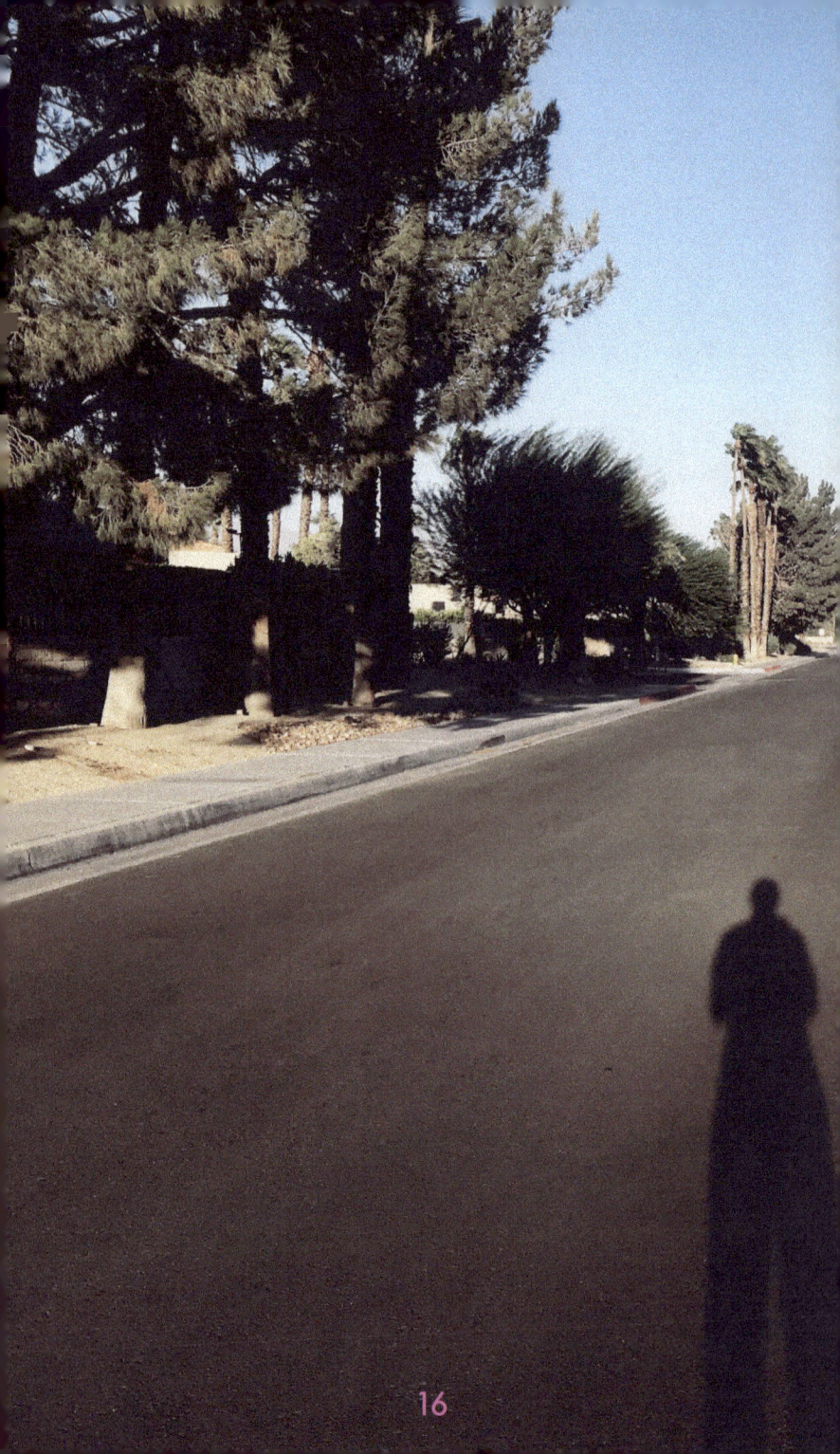

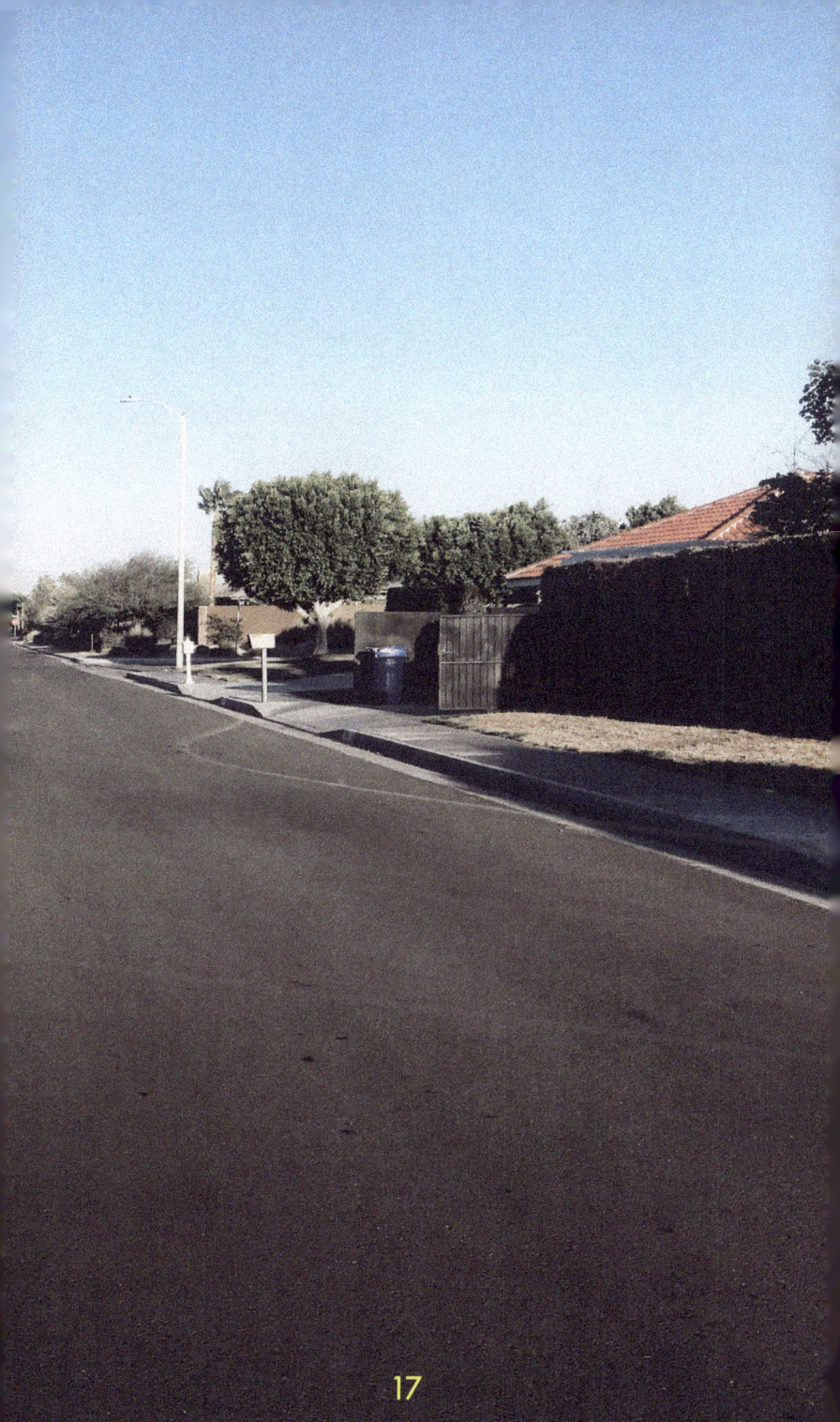

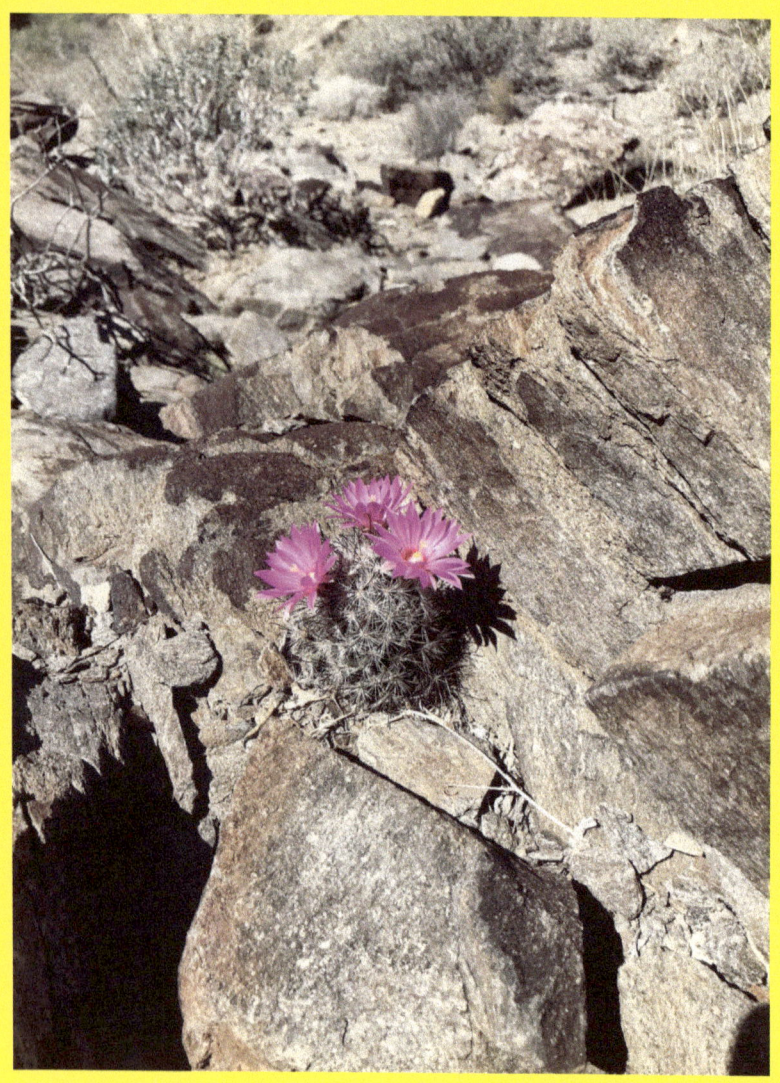

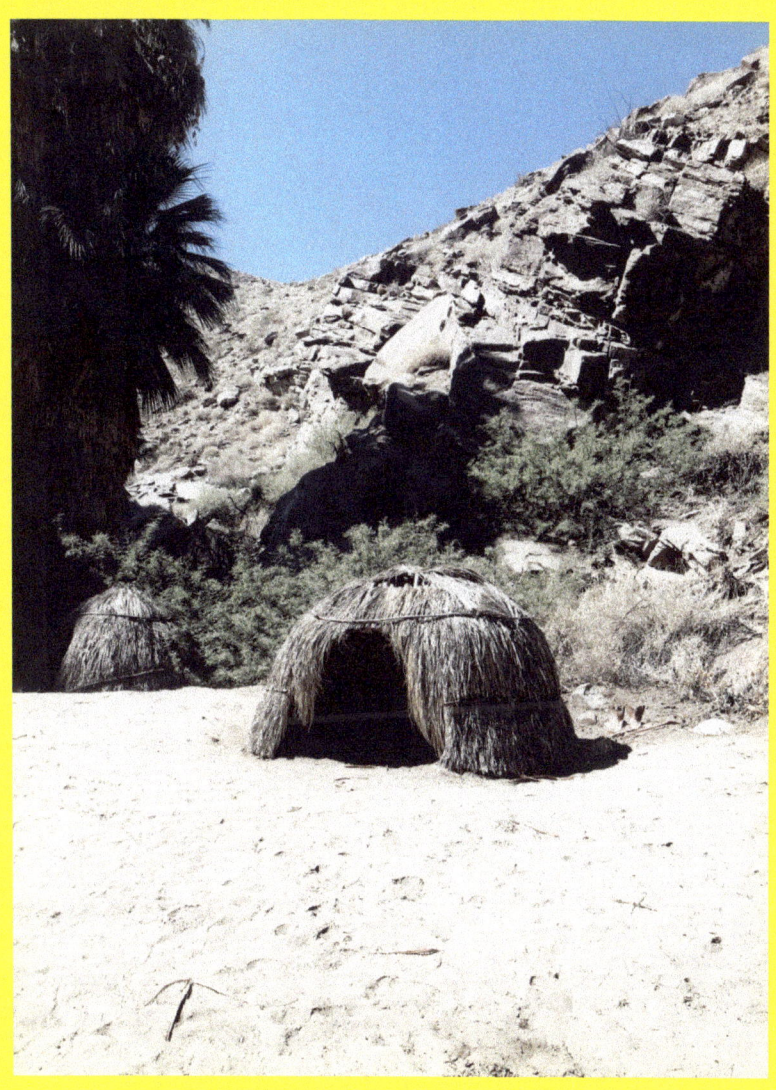

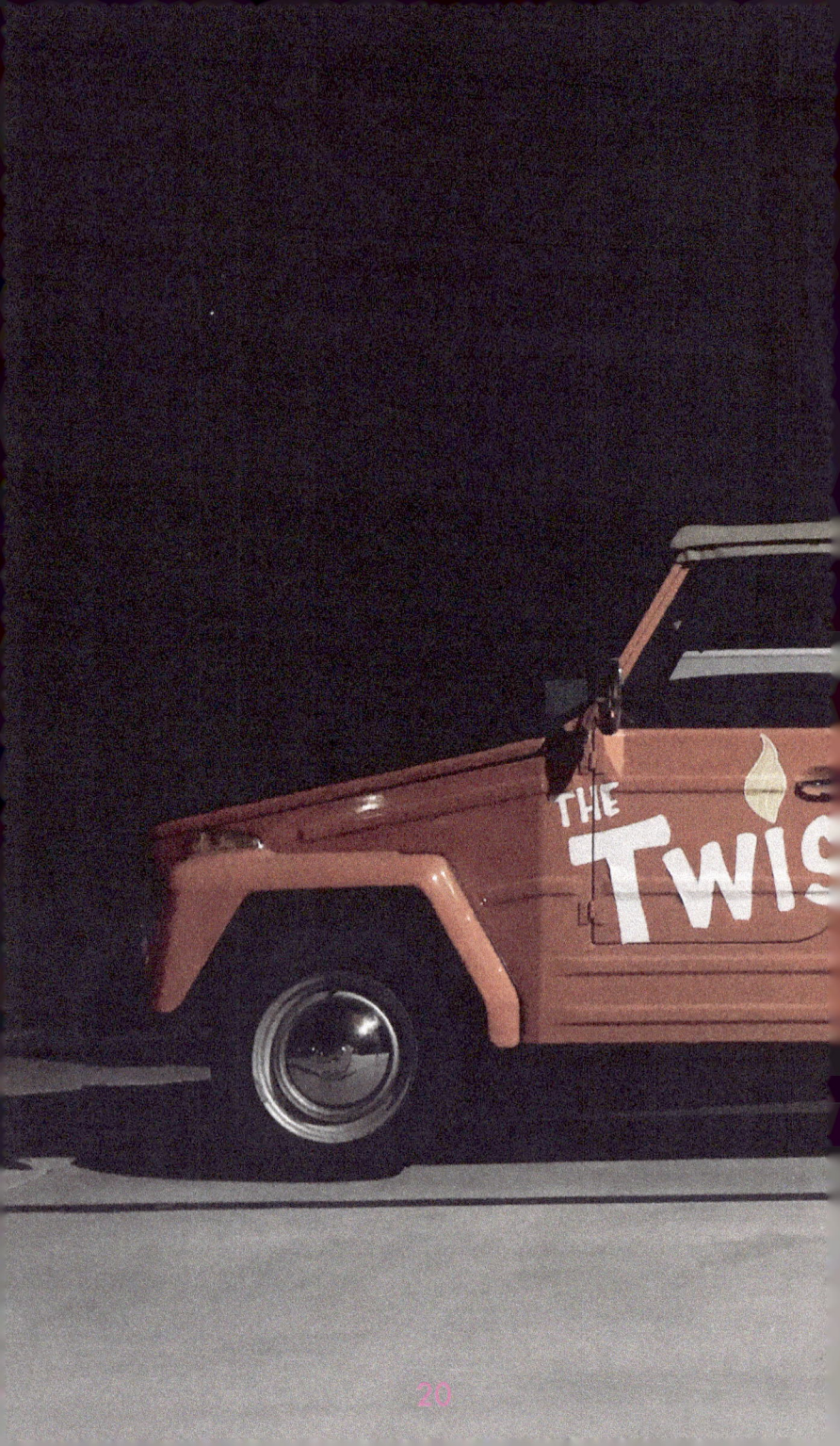

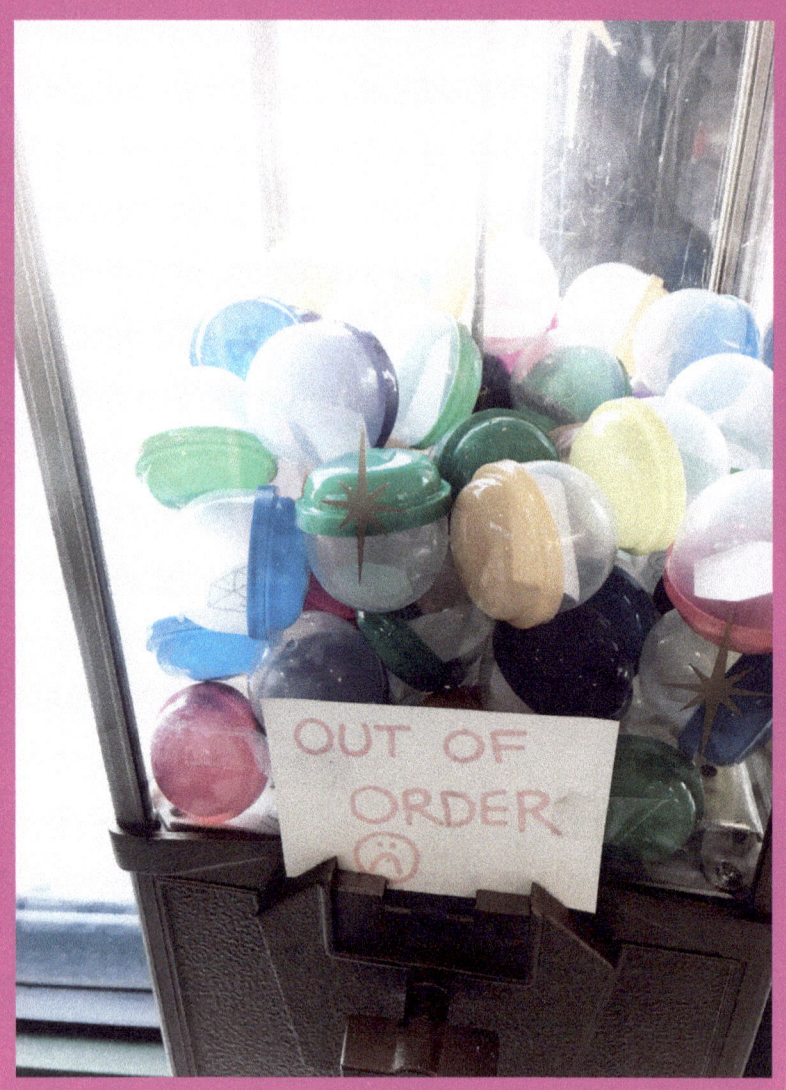

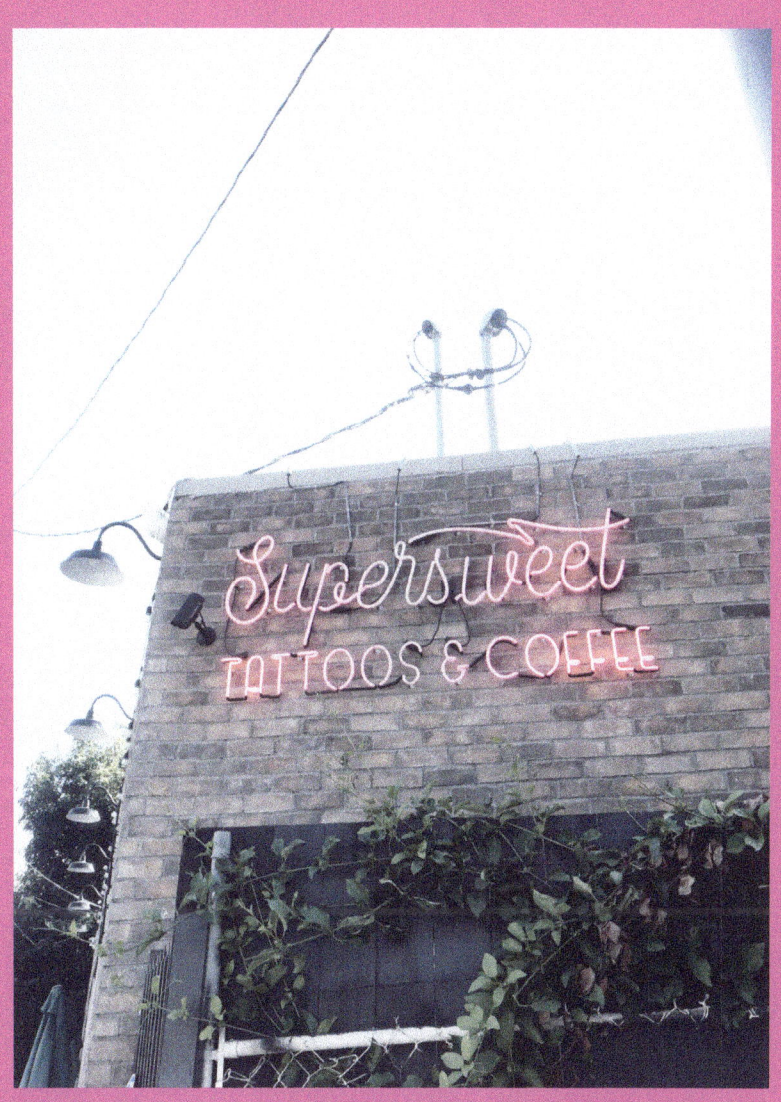

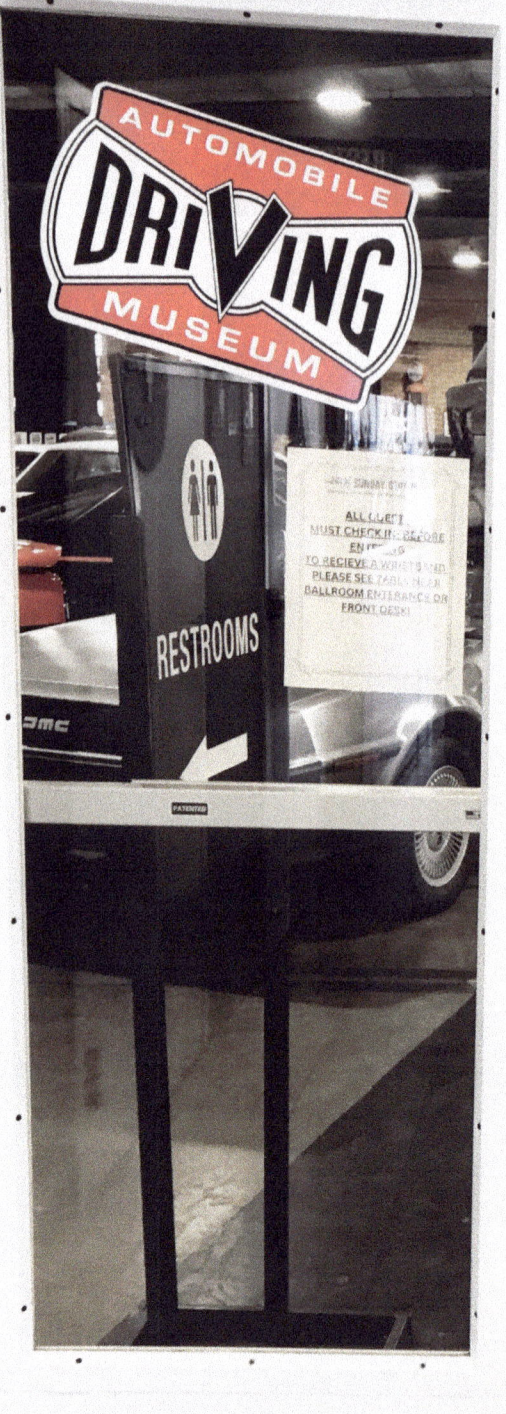

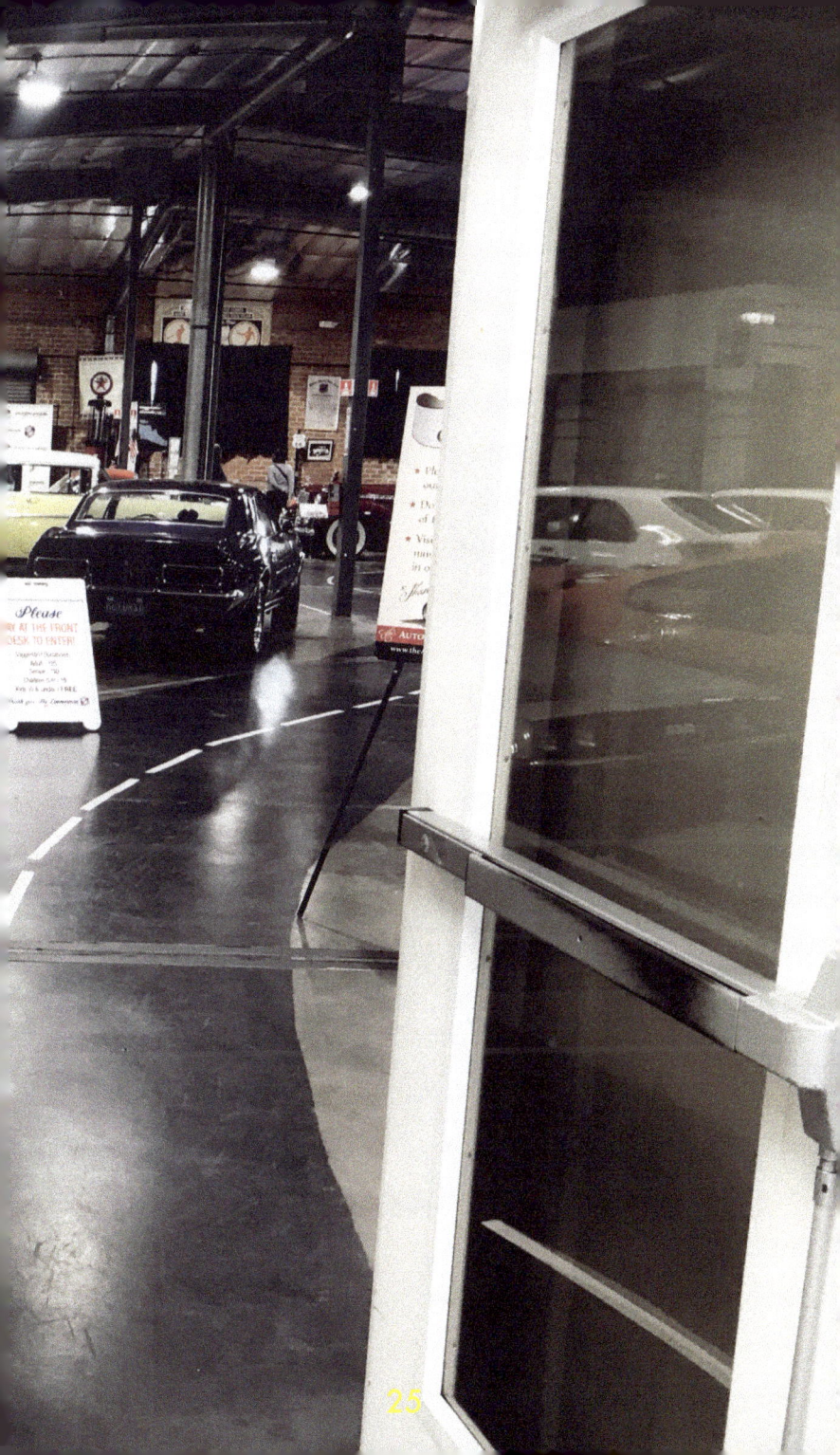

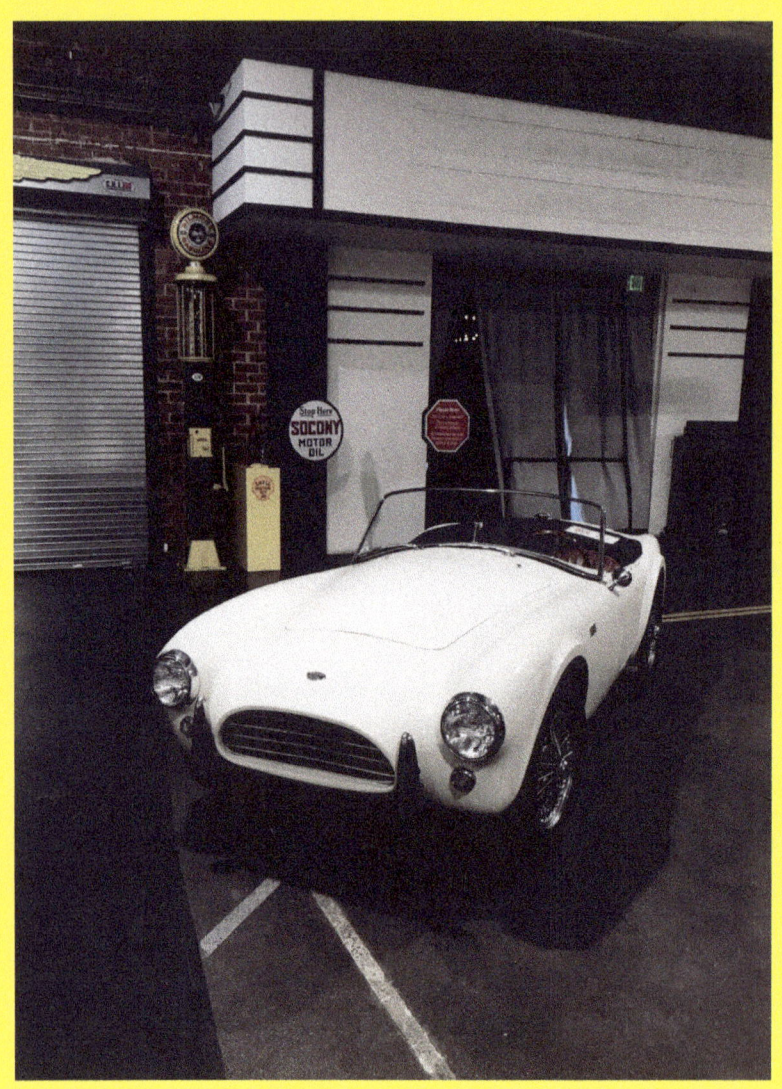

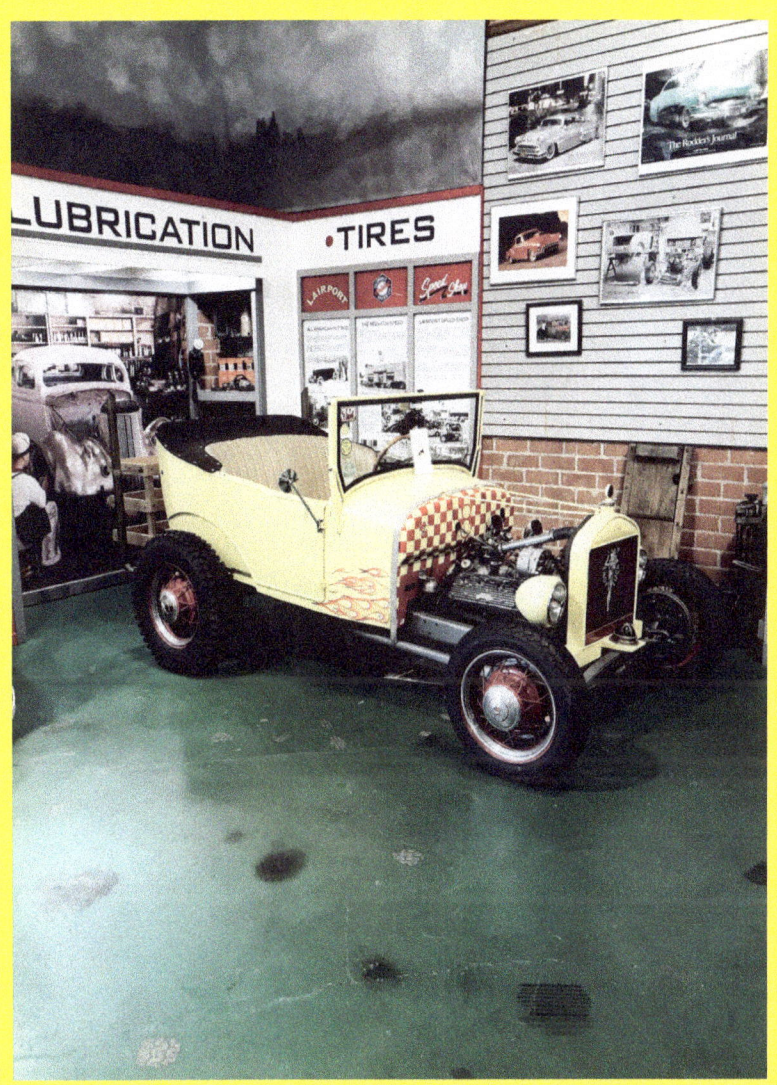

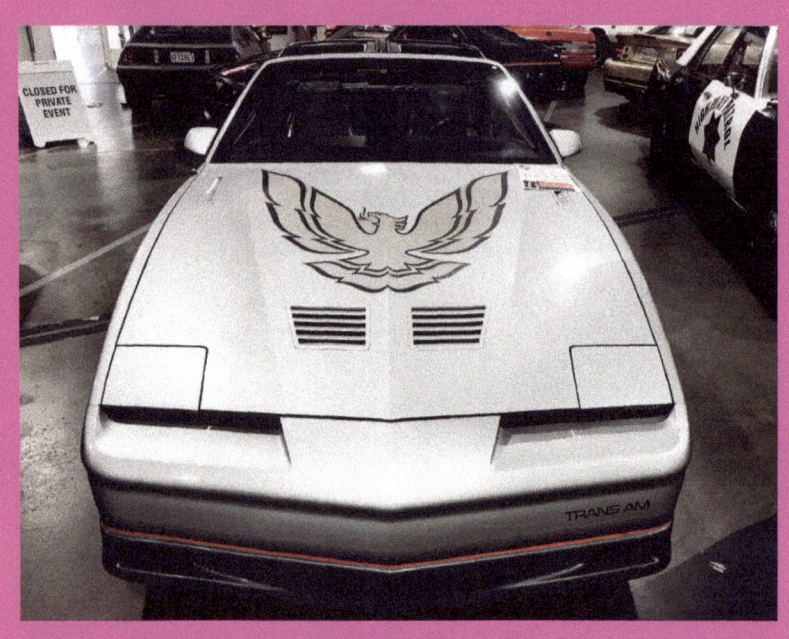

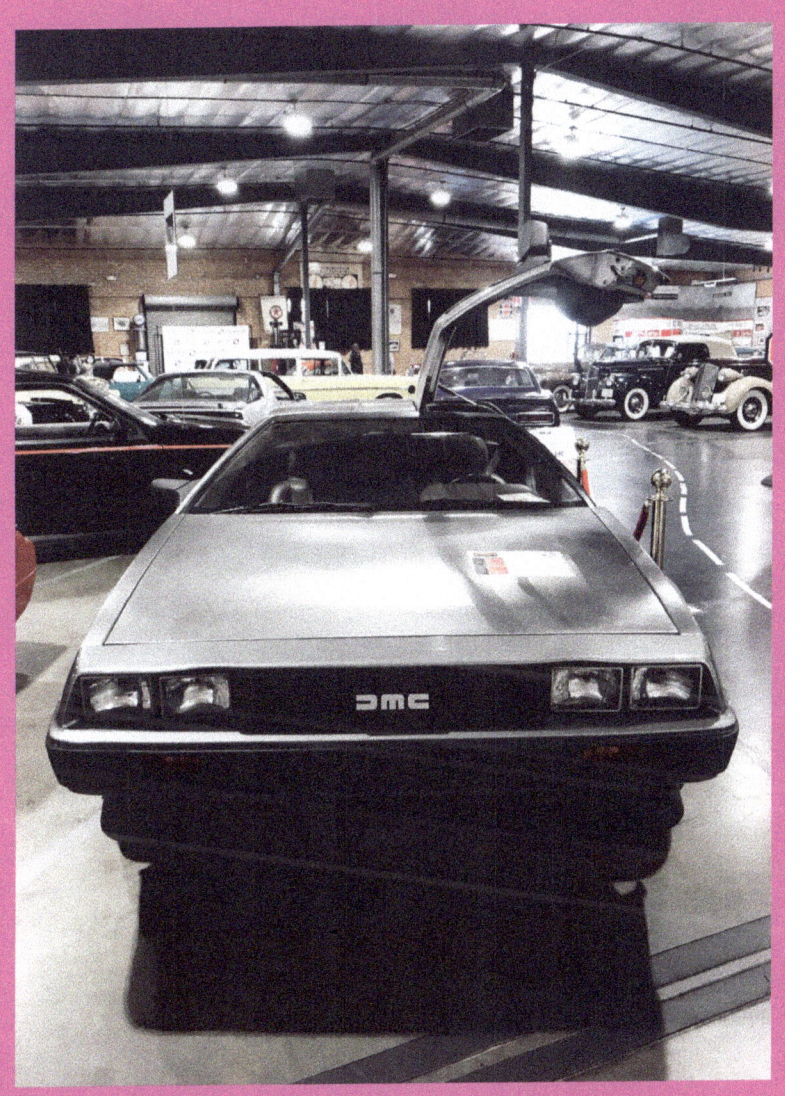

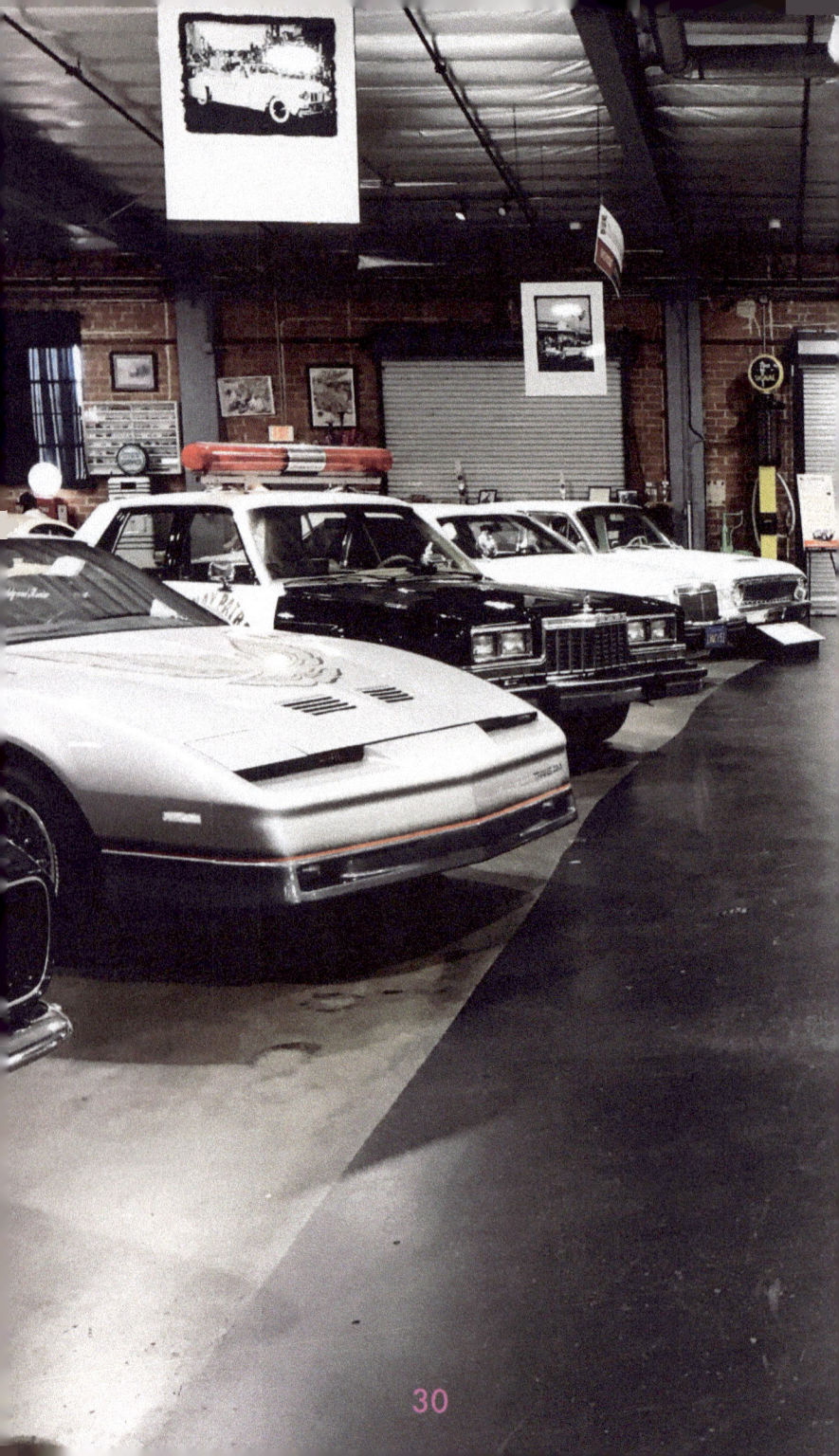

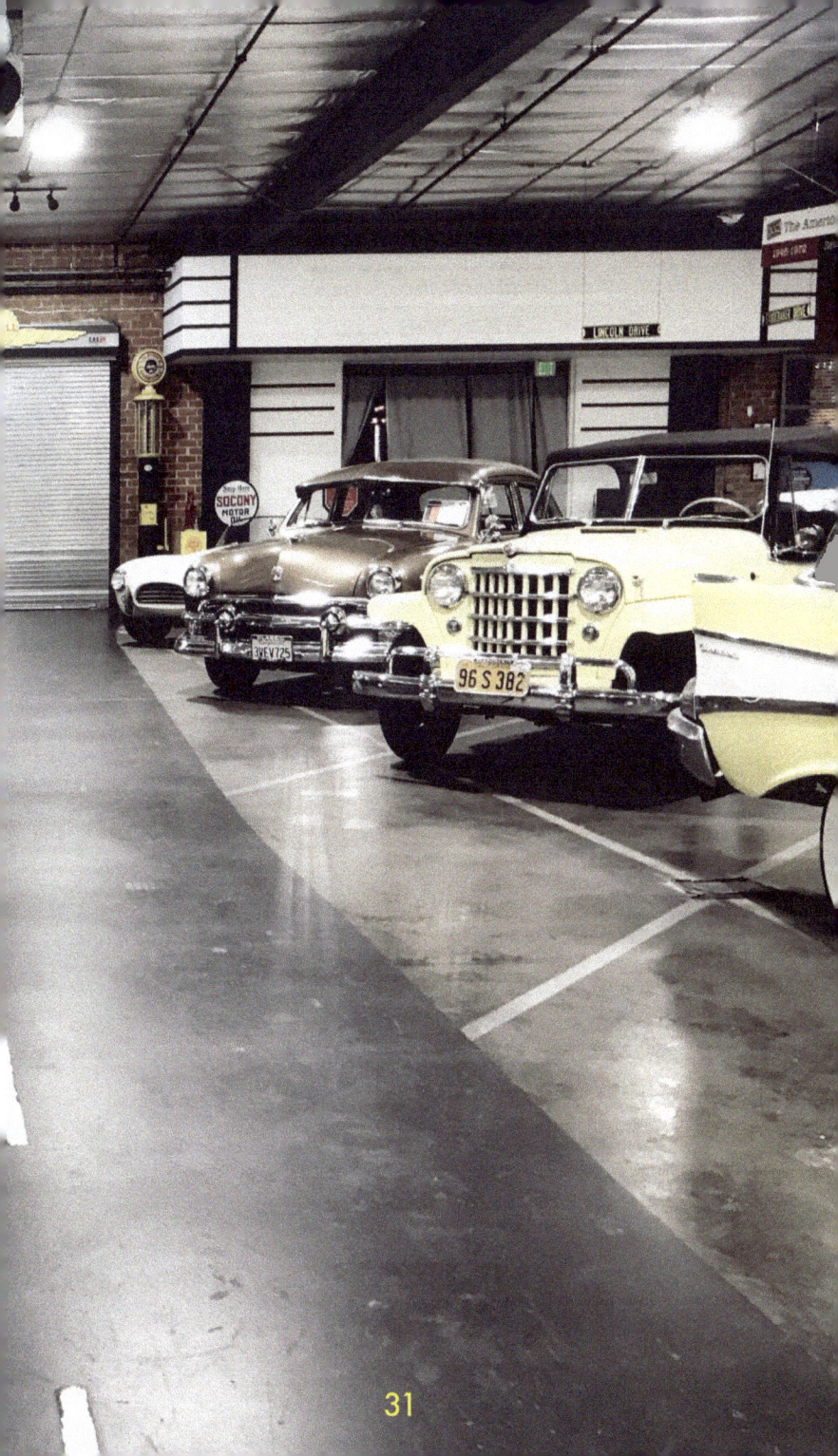

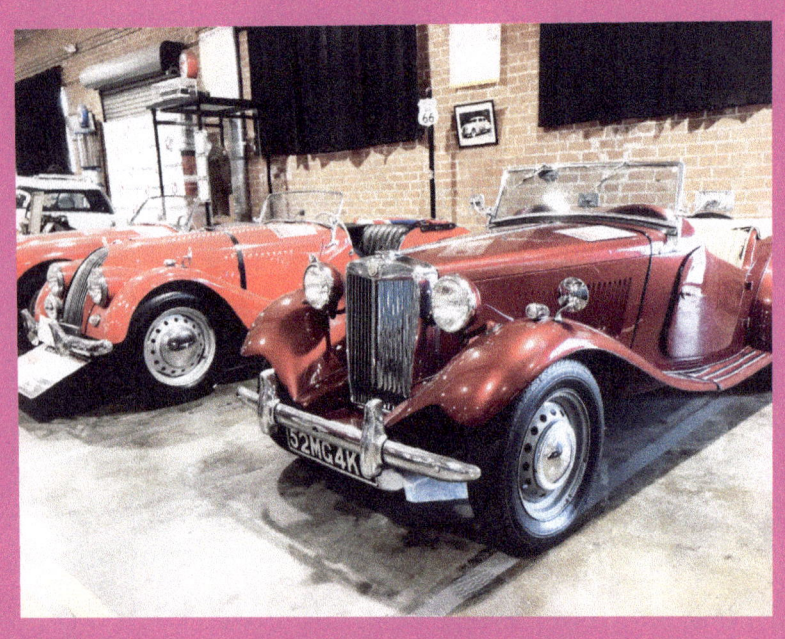

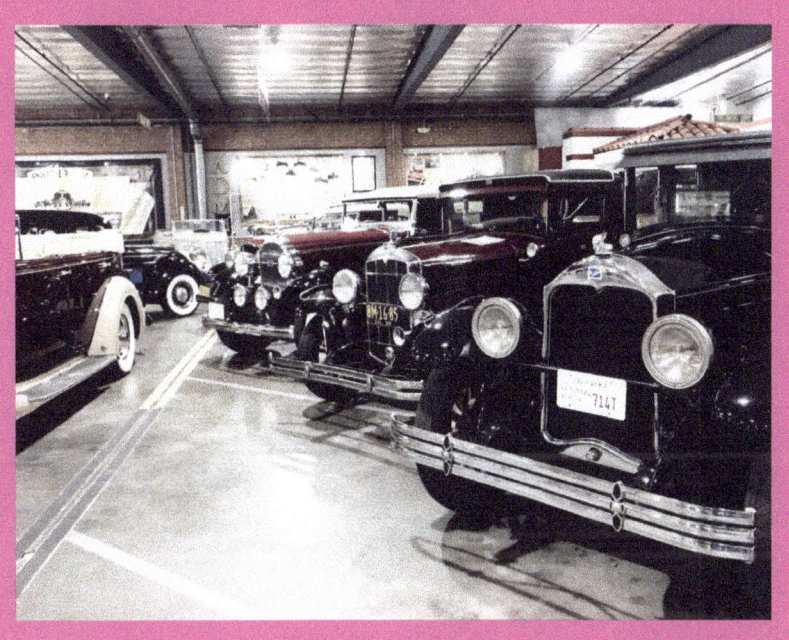

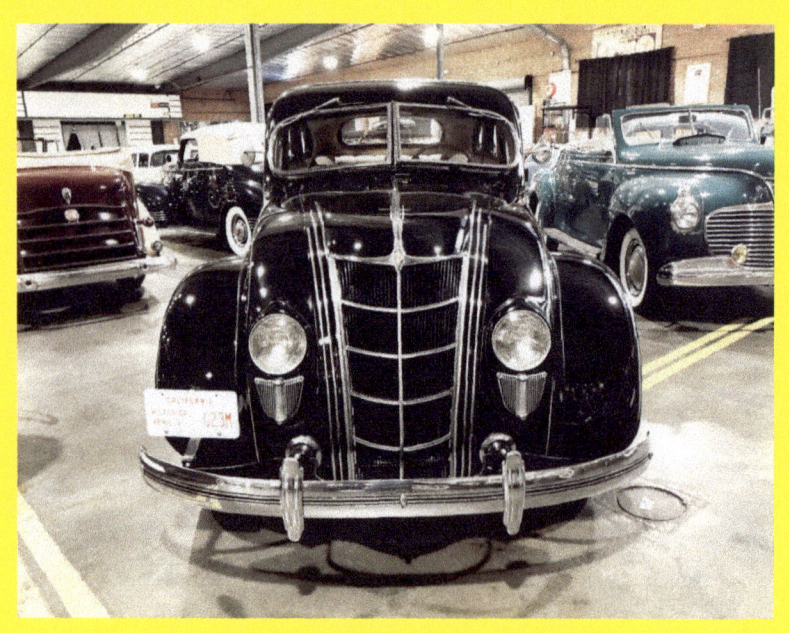

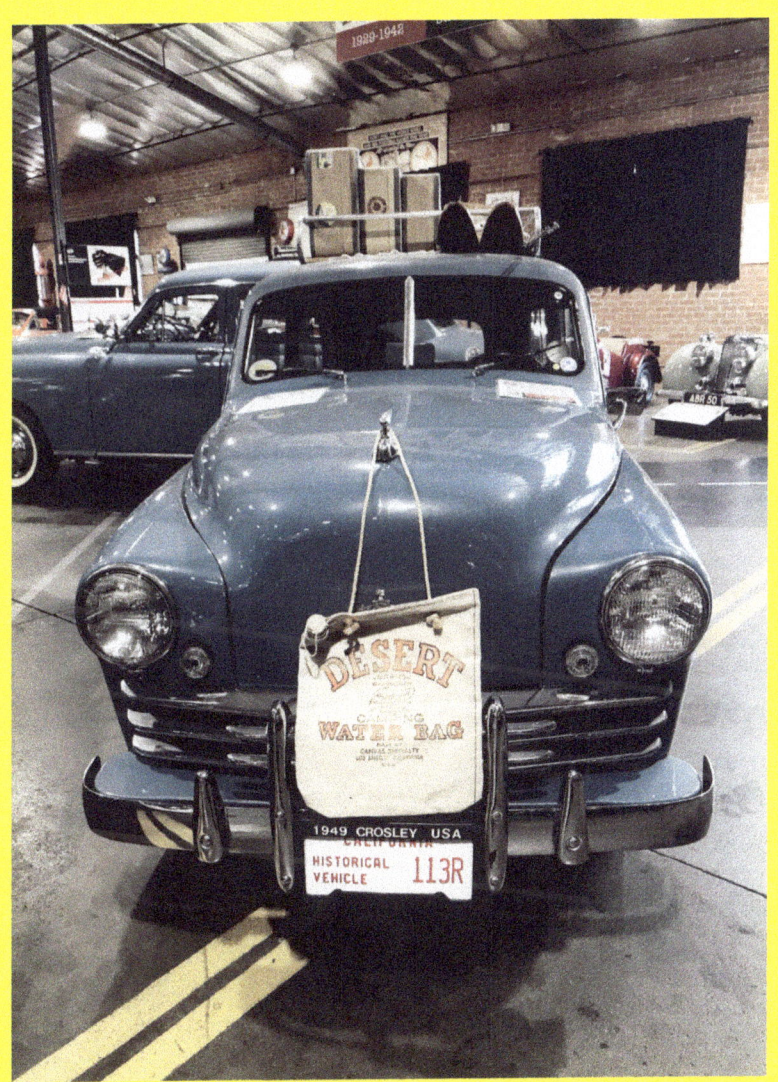

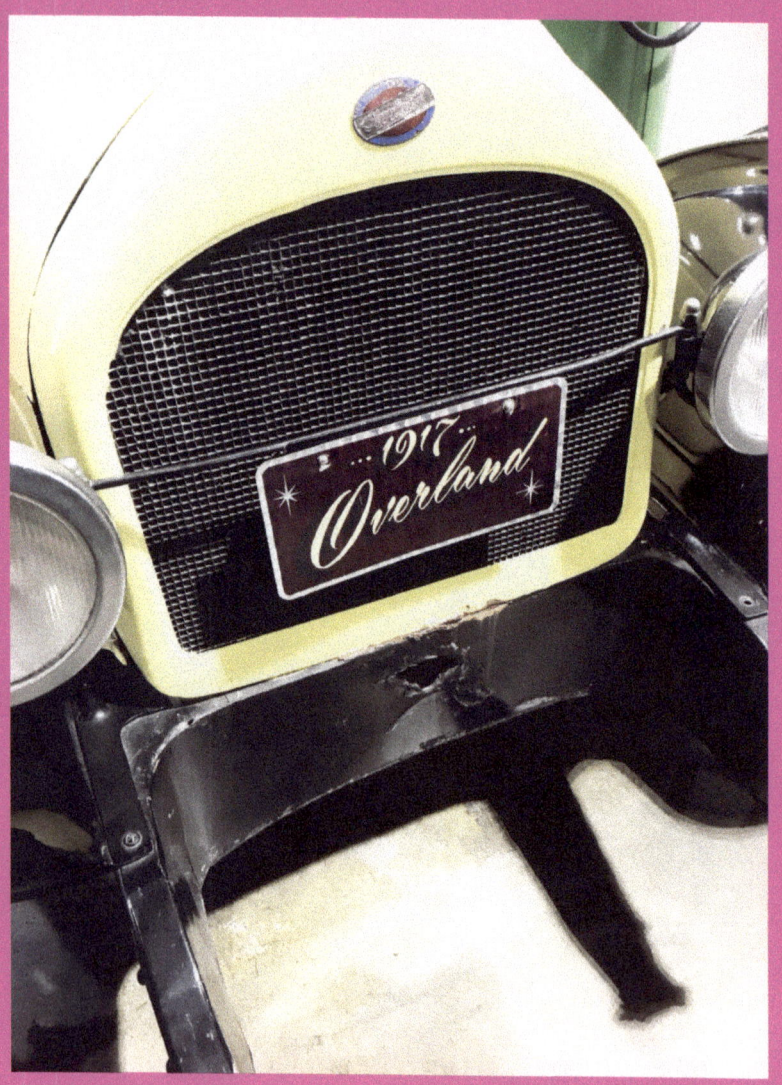

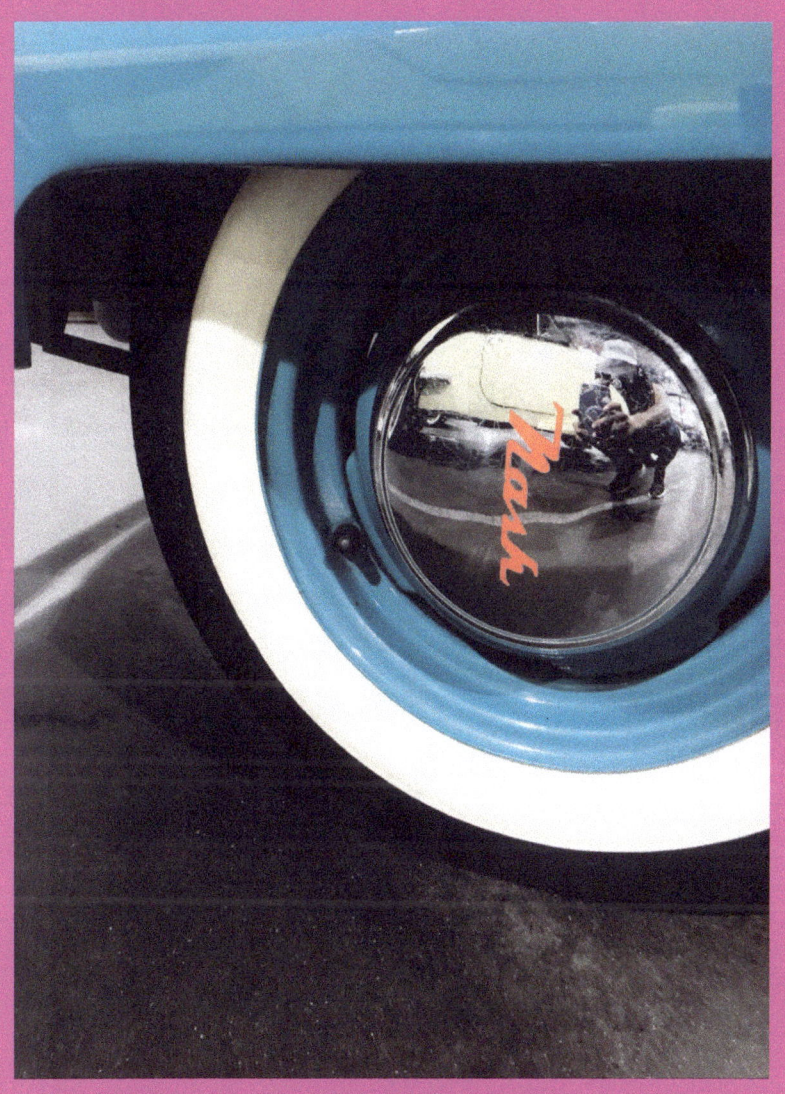

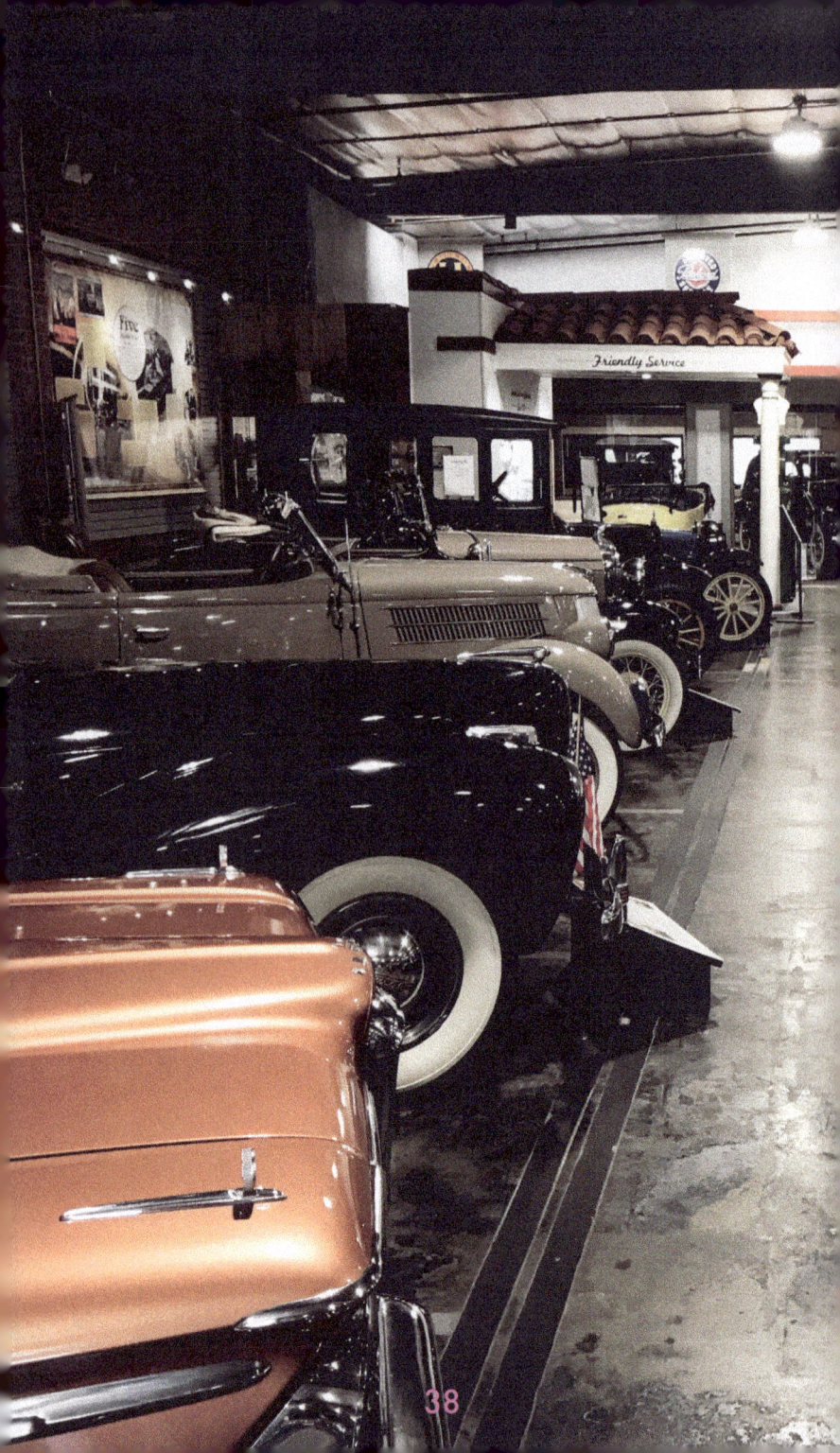

PACKARD DRIVE

The American Auto
Inception to 1929 | From Tiller to

LAIRPORT AUTOMOBILE SHOWROOM

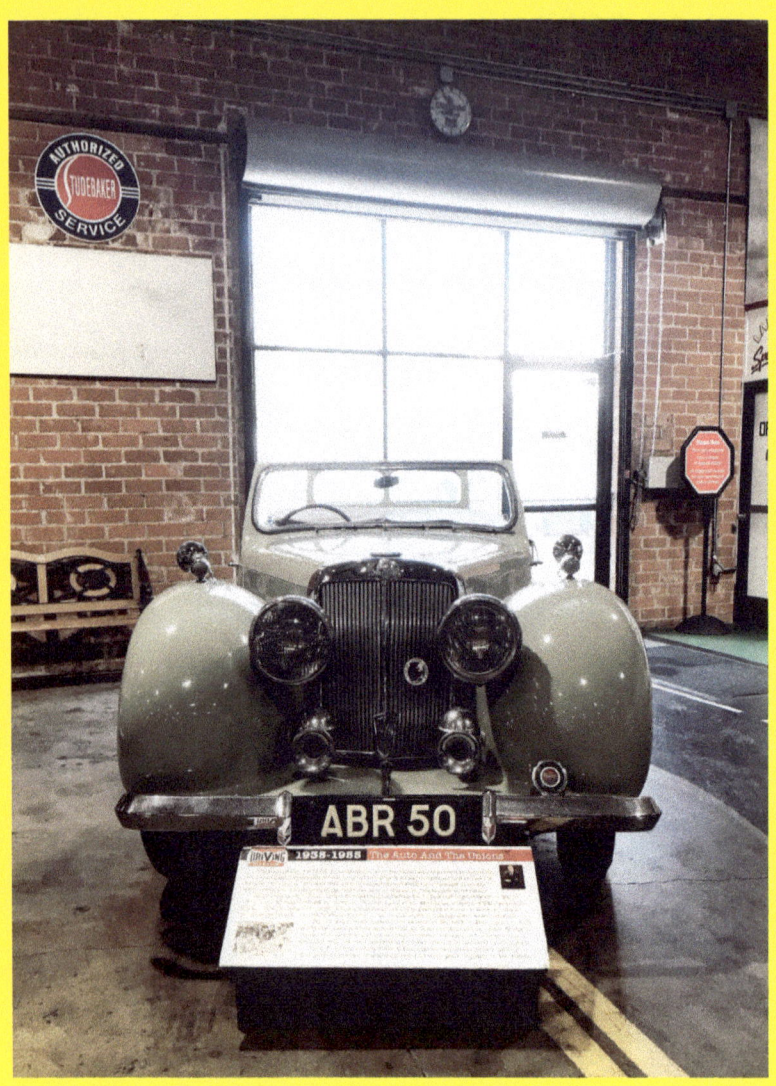

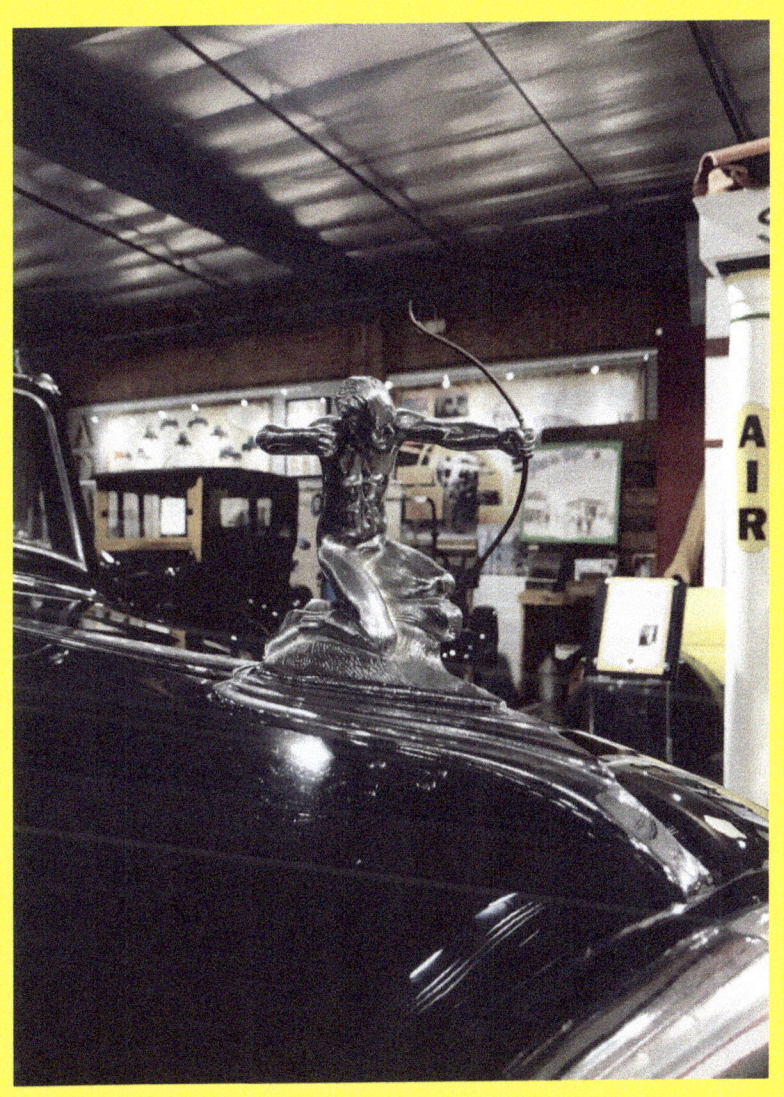

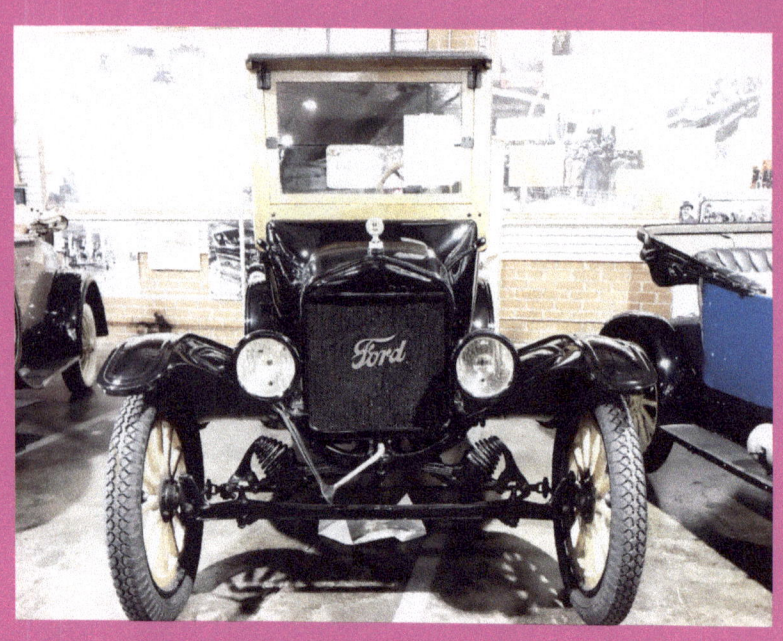

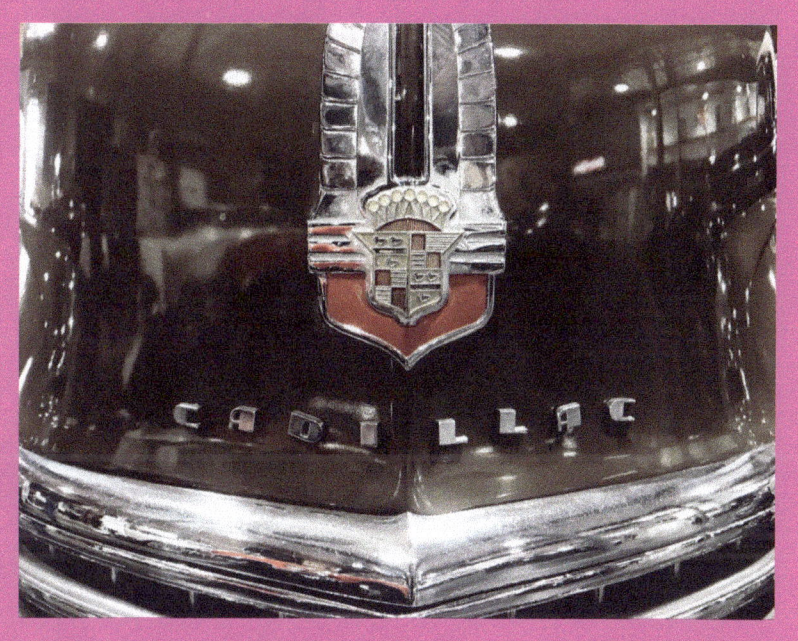

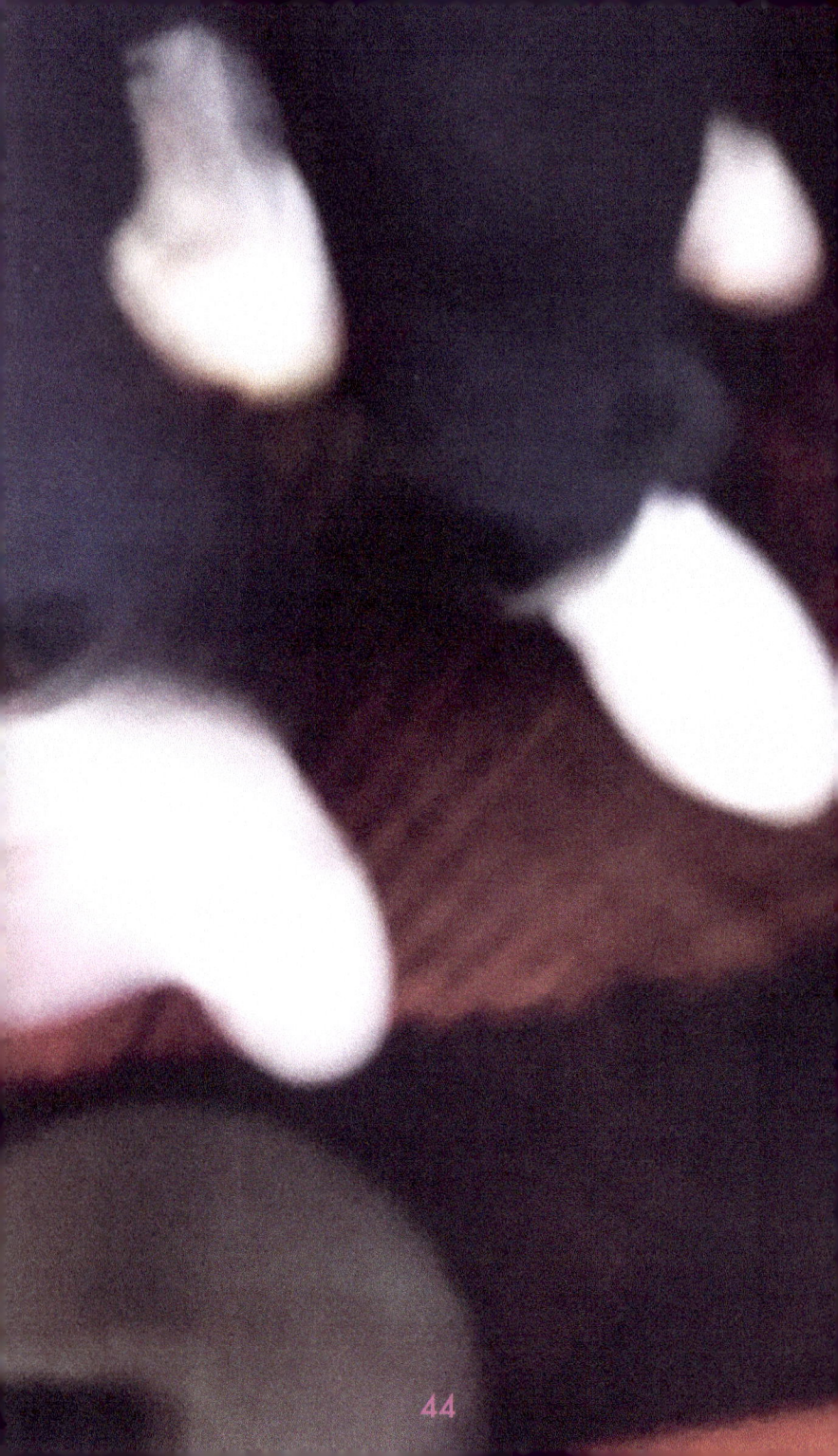

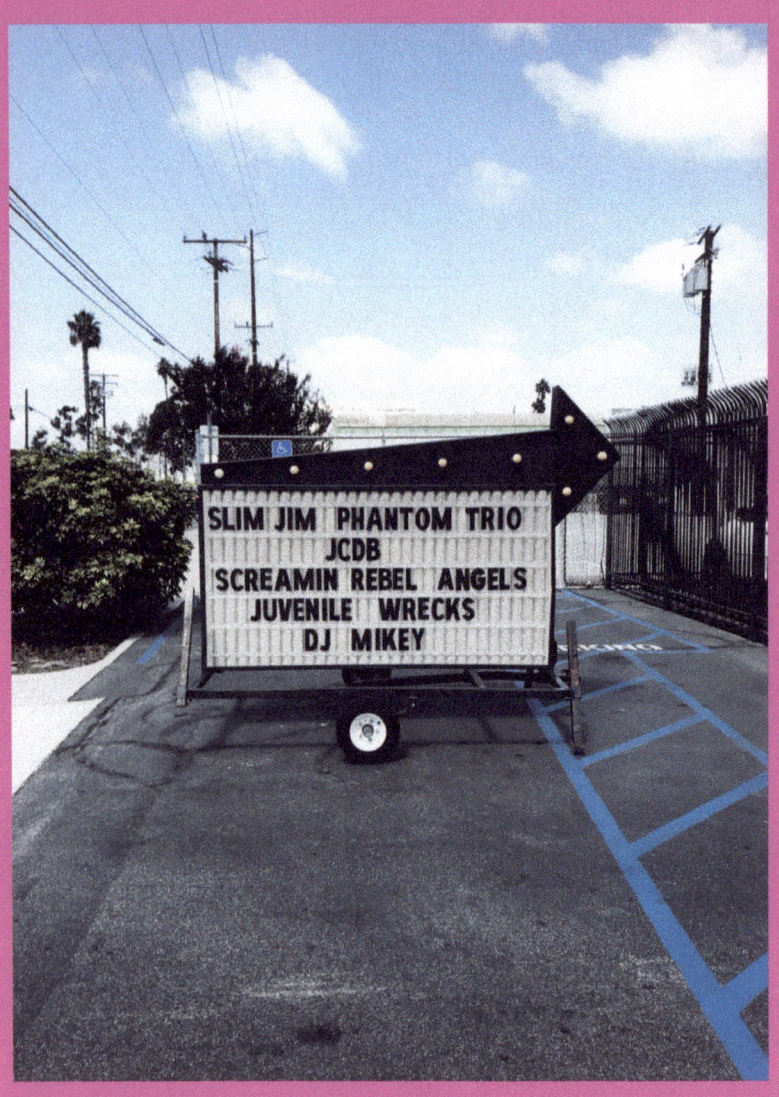

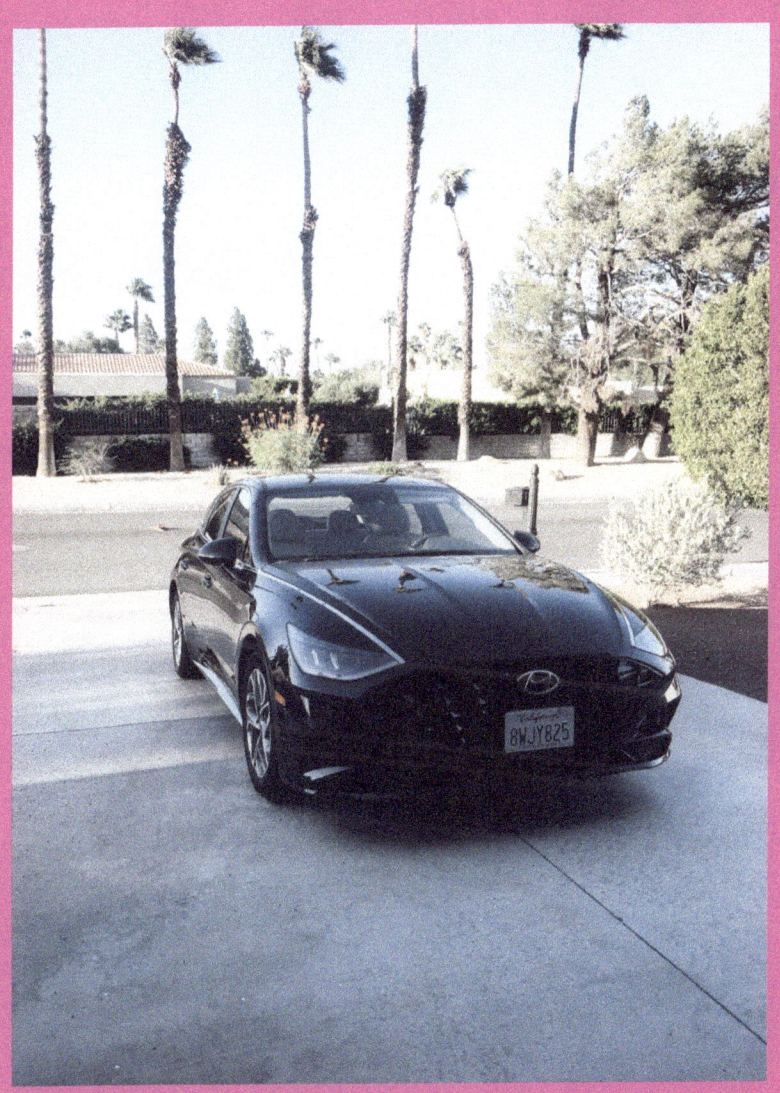

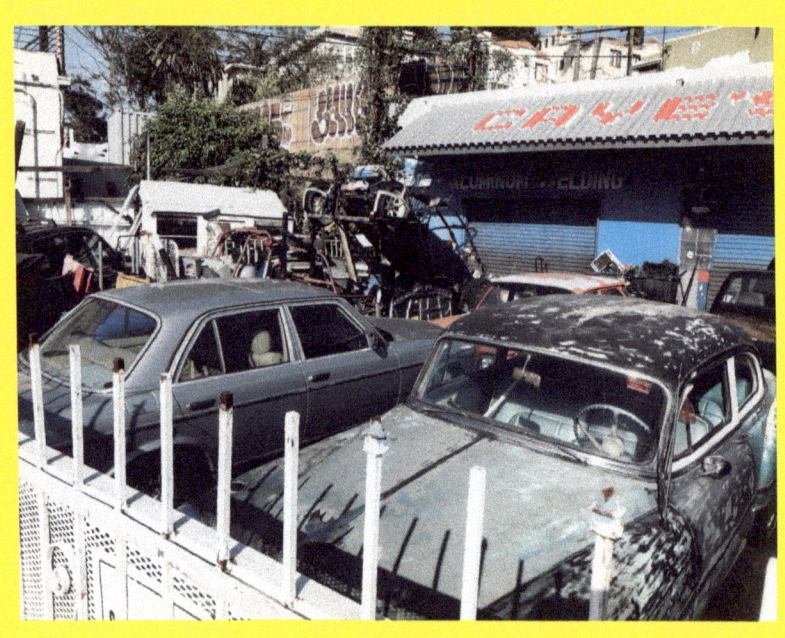

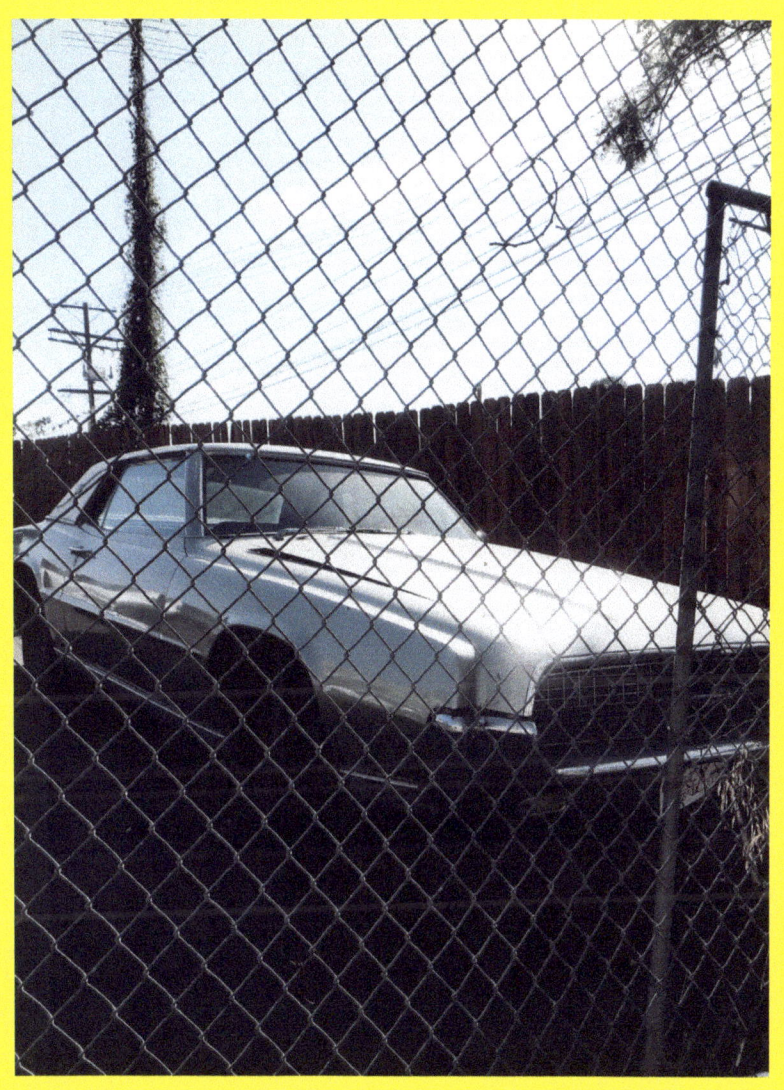

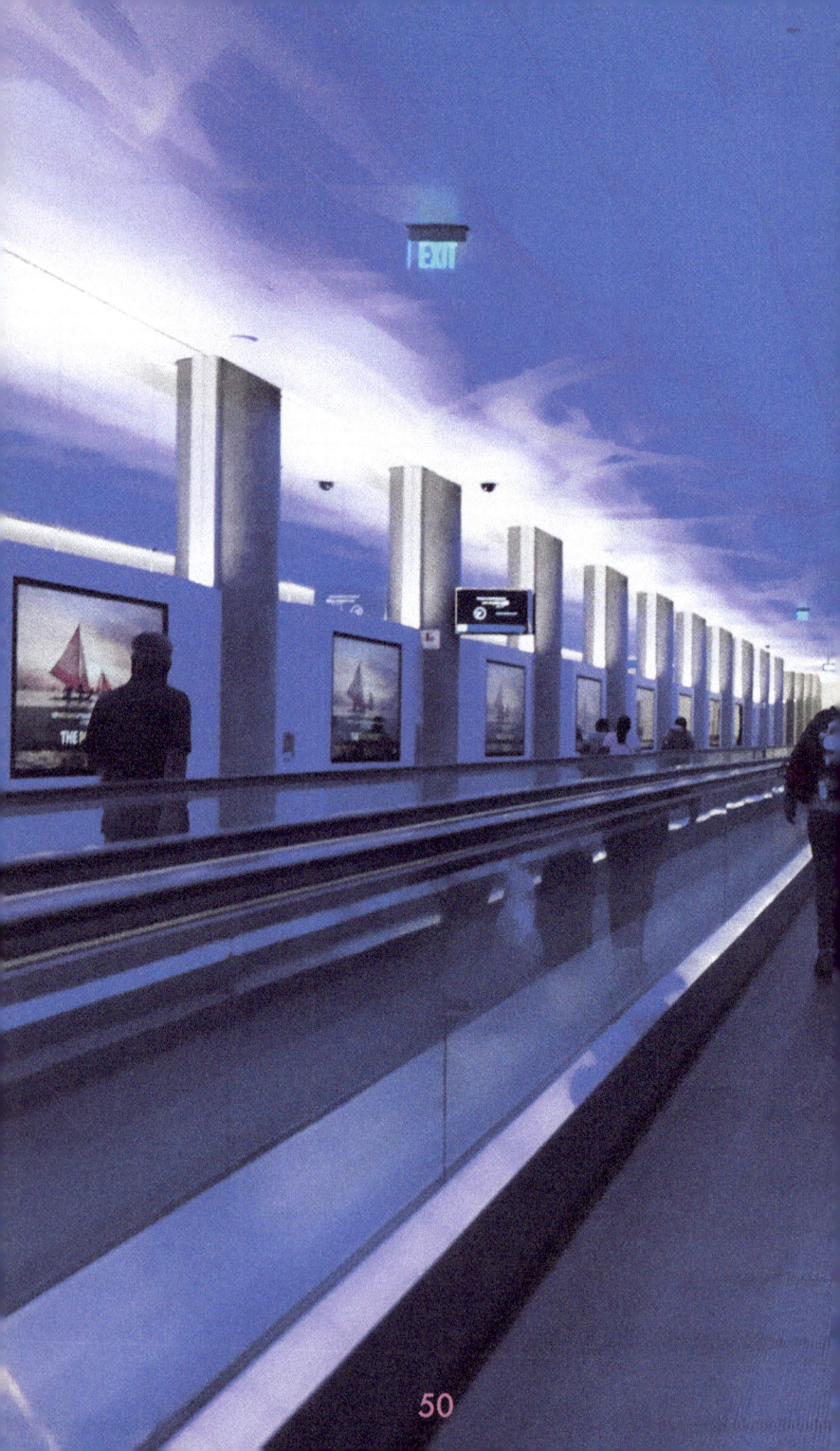

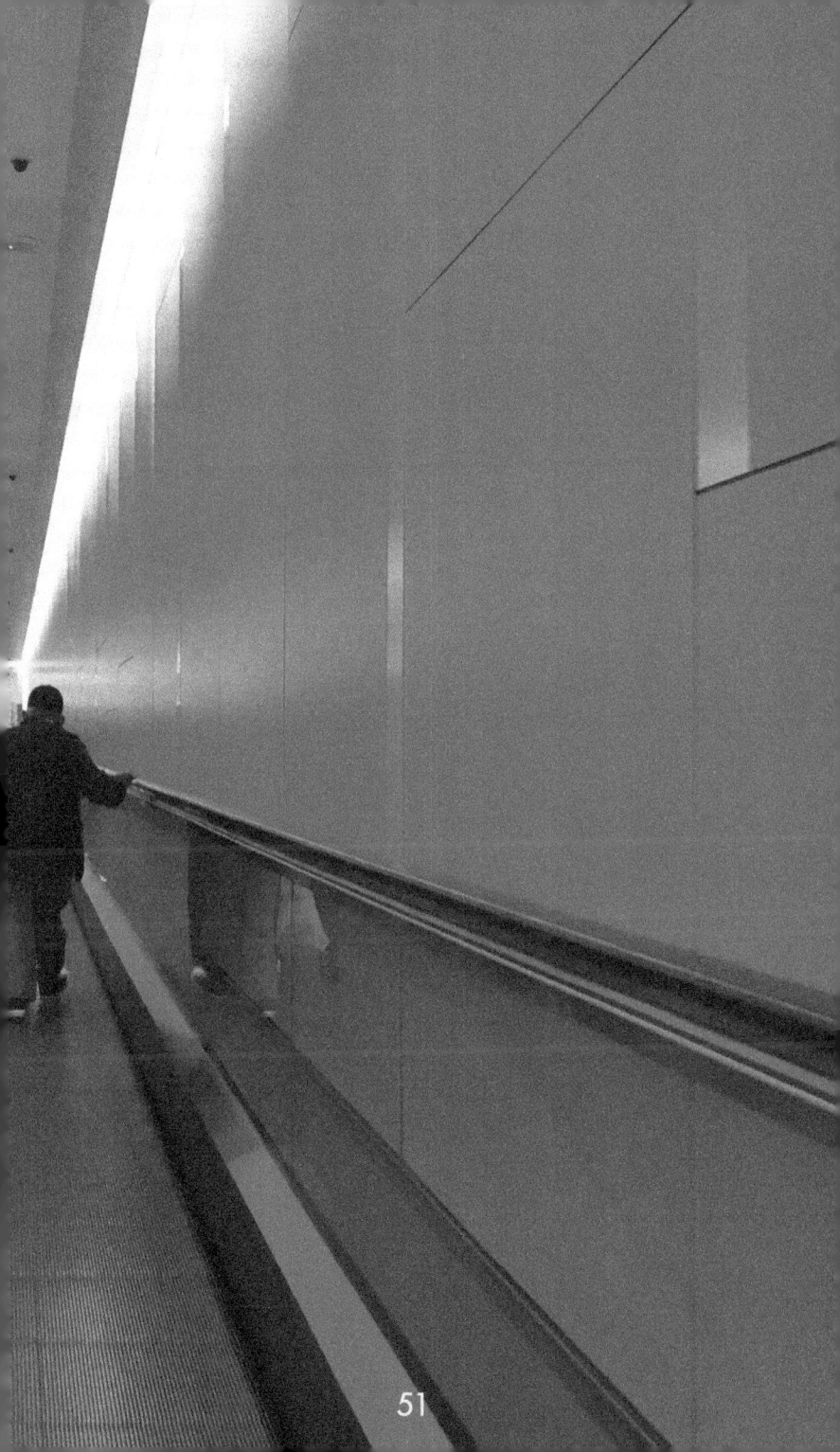

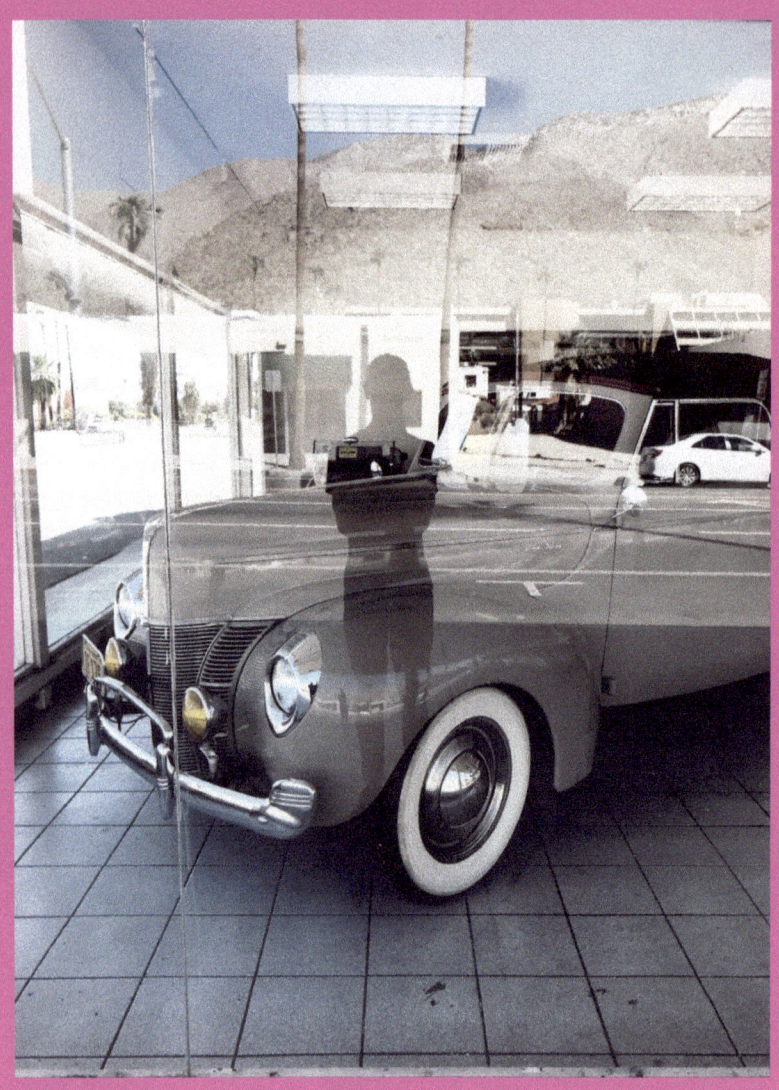

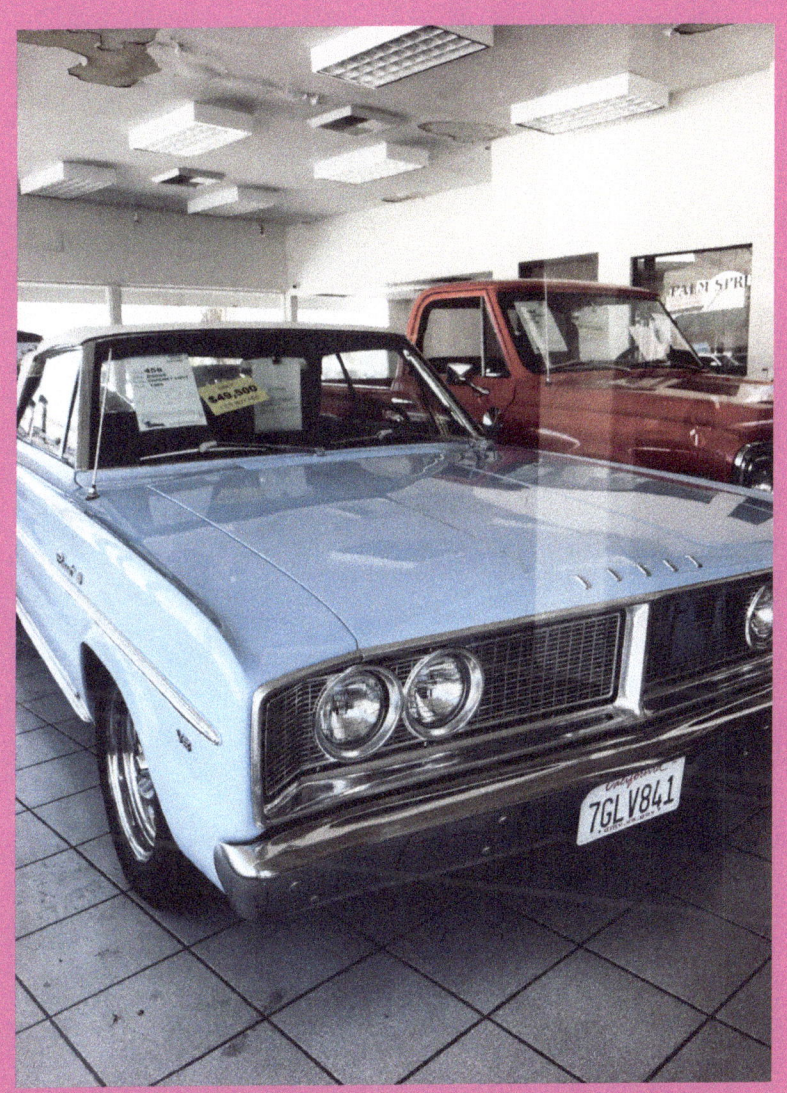

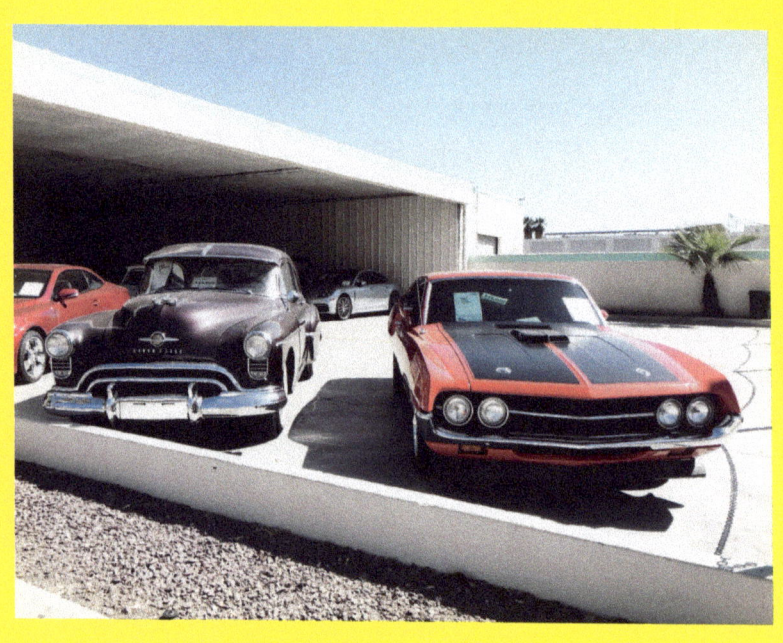

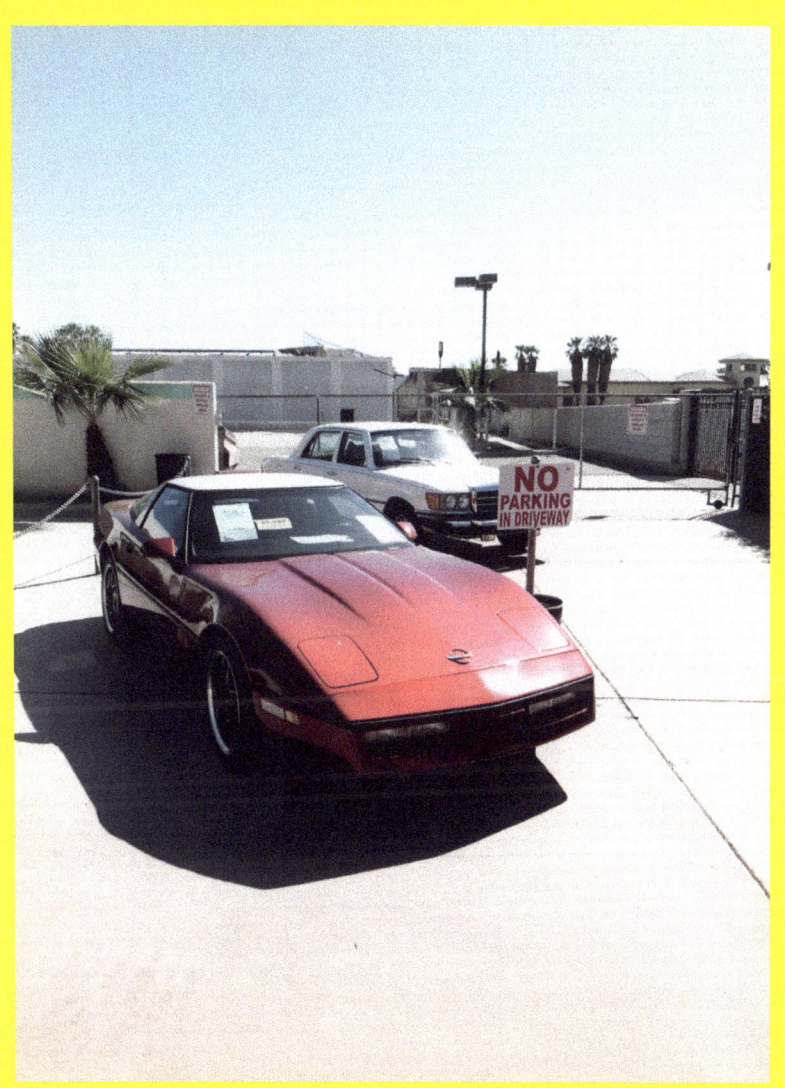

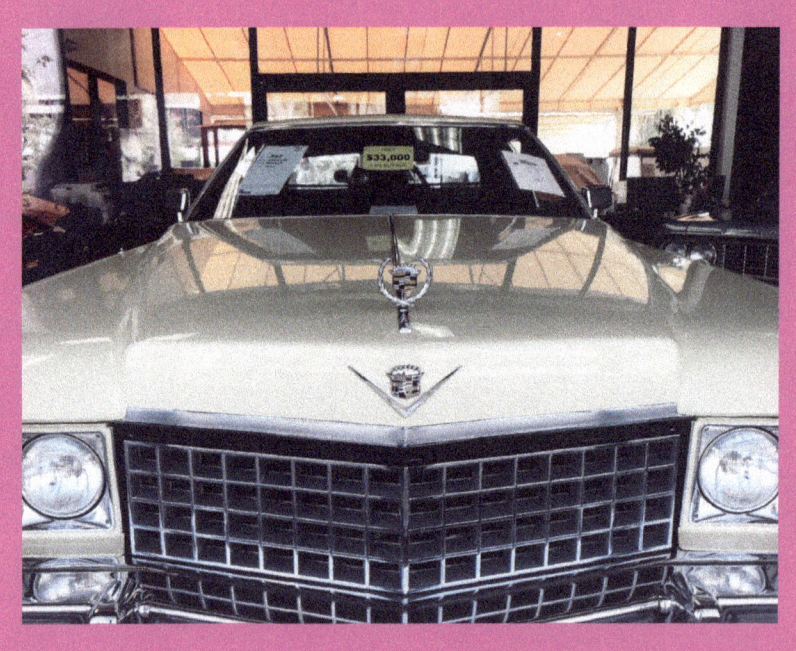

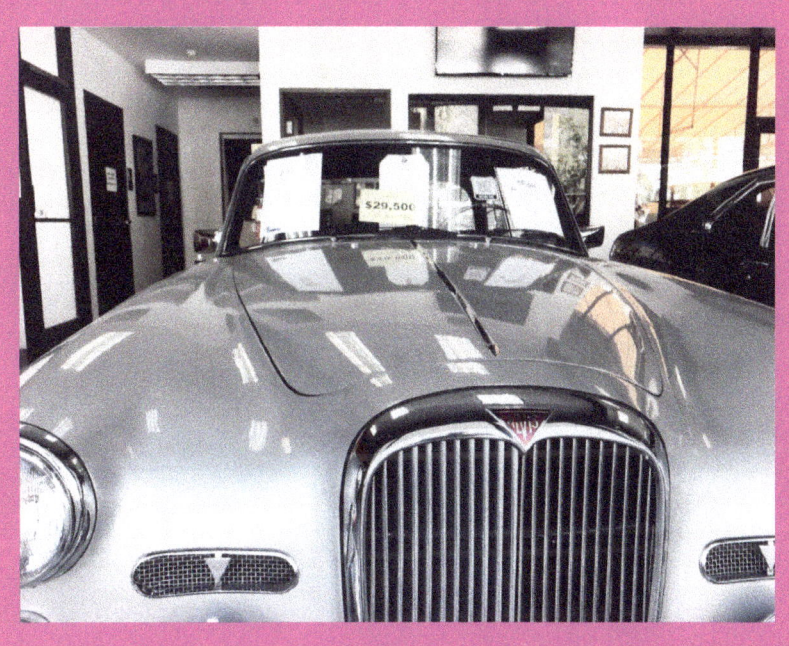

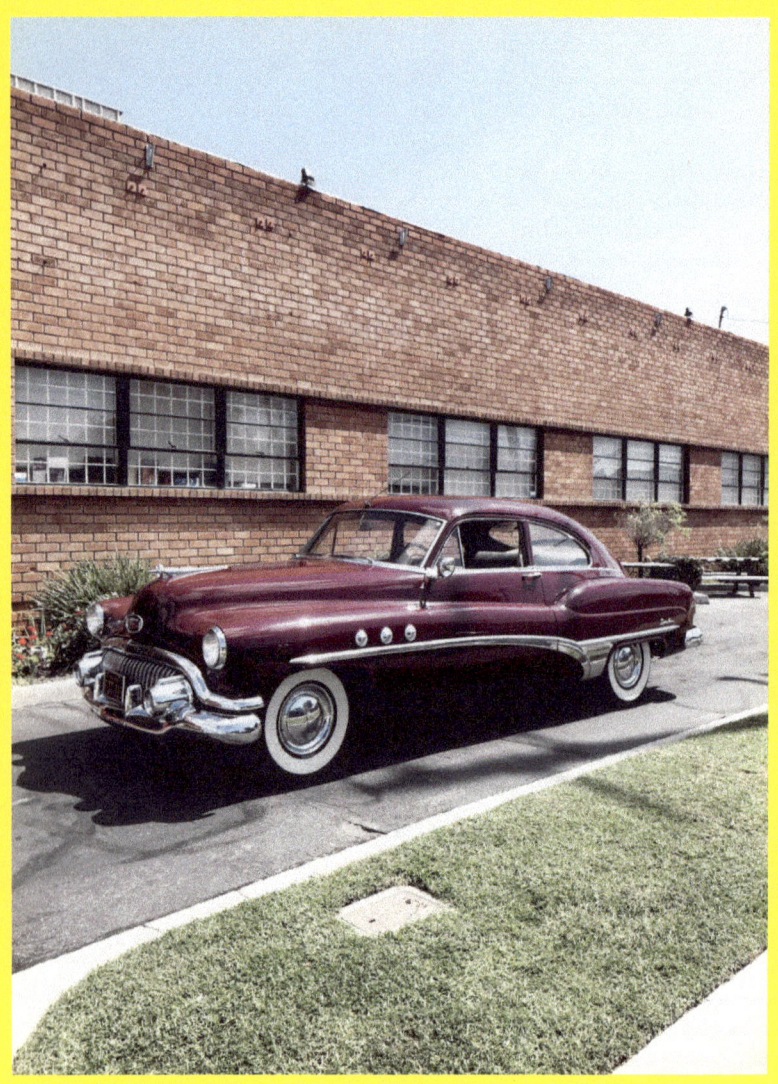

CALIFORNIA

CALIFORNIA

CALIFORNIA

CALIFORNIA

CALIFORNIA

CALIFORNIA

PALM SPRINGS

PALM SPRINGS

PALM SPRINGS

PALM SPRINGS

PALM SPRINGS

PALM SPRINGS

LOS ANGELES

LOS ANGELES

LOS ANGELES

LOS ANGELES

LOS ANGELES

LOS ANGELES

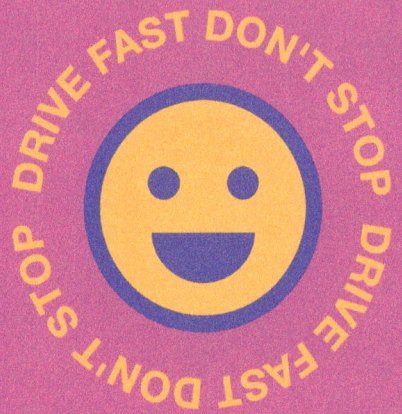

PHOTOS BY
MATTHEW JOCELYN

www.ingramcontent.com/pod-product-compliance
Lightning Source LLC
Chambersburg PA
CBHW040518220526
45473CB00012B/2905